W9-CZU-471

PERFECT
PASTA & RICE

CHARTWELL
BOOKS, INC.

Published by
CHARTWELL BOOKS, Inc

A Division of **BOOK SALES, Inc.**
110 Enterprise Avenue
Secaucus, New Jersey 07094

© Marshall Cavendish Limited 1985

All rights reserved

ISBN 0-89009-819-0

Printed and bound in Hong Kong by
Dai Nippon Printing Company

This volume is not to be sold outside of the
United States of America, its territorities and Canada.

CONTENTS

ALL ABOUT PASTA

Not only is pasta inexpensive, it is also quick and simple to cook and provides a tasty way of stretching meat and vegetables to make complete nutritious meals. The range of pasta now available, both fresh and dried, means more menu variety for family meals.

Pasta is made from a hard variety of wheat called durum wheat which absorbs less water than other wheats when cooked. Pasta is available dried and fresh.

DRIED PASTA
Moisture has been removed from pasta to make dried pasta. If it has been made with the addition of egg yolk it will be labelled *all'uovo* on packages.

Allow 2oz per person as a first course and 4-6oz per person for a main course, depending on the dish.

Buying guide: dried pasta is available in supermarkets; Italian delicatessens have a wider range of different dried shapes. Check the label carefully before buying. The best dried pasta comes from southern Italy where it is widely made and eaten.

Storage: store in a cool, dry place. Dried pasta keeps almost indefinitely, but is best used within 1 year.

Cooking: most pasta should be cooked in boiling salted water, but cooking times will vary according to the type of pasta and shape. Whichever type, pasta should be cooked until tender but firm to the bite, what the Italians call *al dente* (literally, 'to the tooth'). Test by biting a piece.

For every ½ lb dried pasta use about 2½ quarts cold water and 1 tablespoon salt. Bring the water to a boil, swirl about 2 teaspoons oil over the top, then add the pasta and simmer until cooked (see opposite for individual cooking times). Drain in a colander and turn at once into a large warmed bowl. Toss the pasta in a knob of butter or oil and serve at once with a sauce or alternatively toss pasta in prepared sauce.

FRESH PASTA
Usually made with the addition of egg yolks, this is the favourite pasta eaten in northern Italy.

Allow ¼ lb per person for a first course and up to ½ lb per person for a main course.

Buying guide: it is sold loose by the lb in delicatessens and in packages in most large supermarkets.

Storage: keep wrapped in the refrigerator and use within 2 days. To freeze, divide into convenient-sized portions, pack in a rigid container, seal, label and freeze for up to 3 months. Thaw completely before cooking.

Cooking: fresh pasta is cooked in the same way as dried pasta except it requires much less cooking time. If stuck together, carefully pull strands of pasta apart before adding to boiling water. Cook for 3-4 minutes.

PASTA VARIETIES
Pasta may be flavored and colored. All are available both fresh and dried. Green pasta has been made with spinach added to the dough; it is known as *pasta verde* or *pasta al spinaci*. Use for serving with tomato and/or cheese sauces, but avoid serving it with delicate sauces as the strong flavor of the spinach may be over-powering.

An unusual pasta is *pasta pomodoro*, which has been colored with tomato paste. Avoid serving this pasta with red tomato sauces as it looks unappetizing.

Wholemeal pasta is made with wholemeal flour and has more fiber than ordinary pasta. It has a nutty flavour. Use as for green pasta. The widest selection is in health food stores but supermarkets and delicatessens stock it as well.

Pasta shapes are labelled in Italian or English. Also manufacturers use Italian names for their own shapes.

Cannelloni: (1) these large cylinders of fried pasta are intended for stuffing with meat, fish or cheese mixtures. They are then baked with a sauce. Cook as for lasagne (see below) before stuffing, or look for pre-cooked types.

Lasagne: (2) sheets of lasagne are used for layering with meat and cheese to make the classic Italian *lasagne al forno*. They can also be rolled up to make cannelloni (see above).

Lasagne is sold in wide flat sheets and in squares, which are easier to fit into a baking dish. Corrugated narrow sheets are sold and will not stick together when cooked.

Cook dried lasagne for 10-12 minutes until just tender, then drop in a bowl of cold water to prevent sticking.

Fresh lasagne should be cooked for about 1 minute before baking.

Pre-cooked lasagne is an excellent time-saver because, as its name implies, it does not need to be boiled first.

Marcaroni: Italian macaroni are long thin tubes of pasta, **(3)** but most macaroni is cut into short pieces for convenience **(4)**. It is only available dried, either plain or wholemeal. Most often used to make macaroni cheese, it can be combined with other sauces such as tomato or added when cooked to soups and casseroles. Cook short-cut macaroni for 20 minutes; quick-cooking thin-cut macaroni cooks in 6 minutes and is best reserved for making sweet desserts.

Ravioli: (5) these squares of pasta are filled with either a ground meat mixture or Ricotta cheese which is sometimes mixed with spinach. They are available fresh from delicatessens and large super-markets. Canned ravioli is sold in supermarkets; so is dried. Cook fresh

ravioli for 5-7 minutes, or according to package instructions, and either serve with a tomato sauce or toss in butter and grated cheese.

Soup pasta: (6) miniature shapes ranging from star to teardrop shapes. Cook in broth and serve as a simple soup, called *pasta in brodo* in Italy. Larger shapes should be cooked for 5 minutes before adding to soup to prevent it from turning cloudy.

Spaghetti: (7) spaghetti is available in various lengths and widths but is always round. Cook spaghetti according to package instructions. Long thin spaghetti imported from Italy **(8)** and sold in blue wrappers takes about 10 minutes to cook. Fresh spaghetti is available, as is also the slightly wider *tagliarini* or *tagliolini* **(9)** which may be used in the same way. Cook 2-3 minutes.

Vermicelli are very narrow spaghetti, and are sold dried in nests. Cook 5 minutes and serve with a sauce or break into pieces and add to soups.

Spaghetti should be lowered vertically into boiling water and as it softens the rest is pushed down into the pan. Serve with tomato sauces, especially bolognese.

Tagliatelle: (10) also known as ribbon noodles because of their flat shape, this pasta also comes in varying widths.

Fettucine **(11)**, some say, is narrower. These are the best noodles to serve with rich sauces and, in fact, are good served simply tossed in butter with grated cheese and cream added. Serve in place of potatoes, especially with stews and casseroles.

Packets of mixed plain and green tagliatelle are sold. In Italy this is called *paglia e fieno*, or straw and hay.

Tortelloni: (12), cappelletti (13): these stuffed pastas along with smaller *tortellini* are among the increasing variety of tasty alternatives to ravioli now available. Cook and serve as for ravioli (left), or according to package instructions. Dried tortellini is also sold.

Other pasta shapes: bows **(14)**, wheels **(15)**, spirals **(16)**, shells **(17)** or any of the vast number of interesting shapes make excellent pantry items. Cook as instructed on package; serve with meaty sauces. Alternatively, use to make pasta salads.

ALL ABOUT RICE

Countries around the world have long appreciated the nutritional and economical value of rice. In this country we have a variety of rices to choose from – each with its own special use. Follow our guidelines for choosing the right rice; opposite we tell you how to cook it – perfectly.

Rice contributes protein, some of the B vitamins and a variety of minerals such as potassium, calcium and magnesium to the diet. Brown rice and parboiled rice contain more of the B vitamins than other rices.

BUYING GUIDE AND STORAGE

Rice available in supermarkets comes mainly from America and the remainder from India and Italy. The country of origin will be marked on the package. Always make sure, if you can see them, that the grains of rice are unbroken and that there is no sediment in the package.

Stored in a cool, dark place, rice will keep for 1 year.

TYPES

Follow the guidelines set out below for choosing rice:

Brown rice: rice is processed to remove the outer inedible husk. This first stage of processing yields brown rice which may have a long **(1)** or short **(2)** grain. It has a nutty flavor and is more filling than white rice. Use in place of white rice for most dishes but avoid those where its strong flavor may be over-powering such as in curries and paellas. Brown rice takes about twice as long to cook as white rice.

Short-grain rice or pudding rice (3): this is rice which is traditionally used to make sweet rice puddings as well as creamy molds. The grains are fat and oval and become sticky when cooked.

Medium-grain rice or risotto rice (4): these are more round than long, and are characterized by being able to absorb a lot of liquid without becoming soft or sticky. They are ideal for making risottos, which require long cooking.

The easy-cook rice from Italy sold in supermarkets is suitable for risottos but for the best risotto rice look for *Arborio* **(5)** and *Avorio* **(6)** rice sold in Italian delicatessens.

Long-grain rice: this is the rice used for savory dishes. It has clear translucent grains about four times longer than they are wide. When cooked, the rice is light and fluffy and the grains remain completely separate.

Most long-grain rice comes from America. *Patna* long-grain **(7)** rice is from India, but rice labelled 'patna-style' is not necessarily Indian. *Basmati* rice **(8)** is another Indian rice renowned for its distinctive full flavor. It is the ideal – and authentic – rice for curries and pilafs. Unlike other rice, basmati rice must be rinsed before it is cooked to remove excess starch and it

takes less time to cook than other rices.

Parboiled, easy-cook, pre-fluffed or separate grain rice (9): is usually long-grain rice which has been steam treated under pressure before the husk has been removed. The process helps to retain some of the vitamins and minerals which would normally be removed with the husk and germ. Processing also helps the grains to remain separate when cooked. The rice is yellowish in color, but turns white on cooking. Cook according to package instructions and use as for ordinary long-grain rice.

Pre-cooked or canned rice (10): this rice has been fully cooked and coated in oil to keep the grains separate. It is then packed into cans. It only needs to be heated through, which takes just 3 minutes.

Canned rice is convenient for camping trips. It is sold in supermarkets.

Flaked rice (11): here the grains have been flaked. They cook quickly and are convenient for puddings.

Ground rice (12) and rice flour (13): for ground rice, grains are ground to a coarse powder; rice flour is finely ground grains. Ground rice is used in puddings, similar to semolina, and in cookies, especially Scotch shortbread. It is also a good thickener of soups and sauces. Rice flour may be added to cakes and cookies.

Wild rice (14): this is not really rice but the seeds of an aquatic plant that grows in North America. Though very expensive it has an unusual nutty flavor that is wonderful in poultry stuffings. Cook according to package instruc-

tions. Mixed wild rice and long-grain rice (15) is sold in supermarkets and is considerably less expensive.

COOKING

The one golden rule when cooking rice is not to stir it during cooking or it will become starchy. Rice should be cooked until firm but not too soft. Test by biting a grain between the teeth – it should offer some resistance. Allow ¼ cup/2 oz raw rice per person.

Total absorption method: this is by far the best way to cook rice as it is the most reliable. Simply measure out the amount of rice you require, then use double the volume of liquid for cooking.

Put rice and water in a saucepan and add salt – ½ teaspoon per ¼ cup/2 oz. Bring to a boil, stir once, cover pan tightly and then simmer over low heat for 15 minutes without removing the lid (30-40 minutes for brown rice). After this time all the liquid should have been absorbed; the rice should be separate from one another and the grains easily fluffed up with a fork.

Excess water method: this is a good method to use if you have a large bag of rice that has tended to cook to a sticky mass – it will most likely be a poor quality rice.

Add the rice to a pan of boiling salted water. Stir once, cover and simmer for 5-7 minutes. Towards the end of cooking time, test the rice. It should be still quite firm to the bite, drain quickly, rinse under cold water to stop further cooking, then return to the rinsed-out pan and leave the rice to dry out completely over very low heat for about 10 minutes. Alternatively, put the rice in a greased baking pan and allow the rice to dry in a 350° oven for about 10 minutes.

Oven method: this method is useful if you are cooking other food in the oven at the same time. Measure the rice and water in the same way as for the total absorption method. Place the rice and salt in a casserole dish with a close-fitting lid. Bring the water to the boil and pour it over the rice. Cover and cook in a 350° oven for about 40 minutes until the grains are tender and fluffy and all the water has been absorbed. Fluff up the rice with a fork to separate the grains.

Steamed rice: use this method for rice served with Chinese-style meals: cook rice using excess water method above for less than 10 minutes until rice is still firm. Drain thoroughly and wrap the rice in a double thickness of cheesecloth or a very clean dish-towel. Place the bundle in a steamer basket over boiling water, cover tightly then steam for 20-25 minutes until rice is tender. Alternatively, a colander or strainer may be used just as effectively.

Special bamboo baskets for steaming rice are sold in Chinese shops and some department stores. Electric steamers are also sold. Follow manufacturer's instructions when using these.

TRADITIONAL RICE DISHES

Chinese-style fried rice: fully cooked cold long-grain rice is stir-fried in oil over high heat. Season with soy sauce, finely chopped scallions and ginger. Shellfish, poultry or egg strips may be added.

Paella: traditional Spanish paellas are slowly cooked in a special shallow pan called a *paellera* but a wide skillet can be used. Risotto rice is first lightly sautéed in oil, before being cooked in stock. Essential ingredients include shellfish, tomatoes and garlic. The paella is also flavored and colored with saffron.

Risotto: traditionally eaten as an appetizer in Italy, risottos can be made into substantial dishes with the addition of meat and vegetables which are cooked along with the rice. Broth is added to the rice gradually: each time liquid must be absorbed by the rice before the next addition of liquid, which is why it is essential to use risotto rice (see previous page).

Pilafs or pilaus: long-grain rice is first fried in a fat, then broth is added and seasonings. For Indian pilau rice, use basmati rice and season well with curry spices. With Middle Eastern pilafs, rice is first fried in olive oil. The pilafs are traditionally flavored with pistachio nuts or pignoli and raisins.

APPETIZERS

Minestrone

Italian Minestrone is one of the world's great soups. Made from different mixed vegetables with cooked dried peas or beans and either small pasta shapes or rice added, it is a thick soup that is nourishing and filling.

A warming bowlful of minestrone sprinkled with grated Parmesan cheese is perfect for a cold wintry day, but in fact it was originally a summer soup. Equally good served hot or cold (but not chilled), it always seems to taste even better the day after it is made. For the very best flavor, do not serve the soup piping hot, but allow it to cool slightly first so that the flavor has time to develop and 'mature'.

The secret of good minestrone is to use really fresh vegetables which are cooked in olive oil to start with (the Italians call this stage *soffrito*), then simmered very gently for a long time so that all their goodness and flavor come through. Frozen vegetables should not be used for making minestrone: they give unsatisfactory results.

SERVES 8
2 tablespoons olive oil (see Did you know)
2 lean bacon slices finely chopped
2 tablespoons chopped parsley
1 clove garlic, finely chopped
3 cups roughly shredded cabbage, (see Preparation)
¼ lb spinach, cut into small, thin strips (see Preparation)
1 large potato, diced
1 large zucchini, sliced
1 carrot, diced
1 onion, chopped
1 celery stalk, sliced

Cook's Notes

 TIME
Preparation and preliminary cooking take about 45 minutes. Cooking takes about 1¾ hours. Allow 10-15 minutes for the soup to cool slightly before serving.

 DID YOU KNOW
The finest Italian olive oil is said to come from Lucca in Tuscany and Sassari in Sardinia. Dark green in color and fruity in flavor, these are the best oils to use when cooking Italian food, for the most authentic flavor. They are available at supermarkets and Italian delicatessens.

BUYING GUIDE
Any small pasta shapes, such as stars or letters of the alphabet, for example, would look attractive.

 PREPARATION
After shredding the cabbage and spinach, make sure they are absolutely dry by patting thoroughly with absorbent kitchen paper: any water left on the shredded leaves would interfere with the cooking process.

FREEZING
Make the soup up to the end of stage 4, cool quickly and skim off any fat from the surface. Pour into rigid containers, leaving 1 inch headspace, cover, label and freeze for up to 3 months. To serve: reheat gently from frozen, adding a little water if the soup sticks to the pan at first. Then proceed from the beginning of stage 5.

●320 calories per portion

1 can (about 1 lb) chopped tomatoes
2½ quarts vegetable or chicken broth
salt and freshly ground black pepper
1 cup small pasta shells or elbow macaroni (see Buying guide)
1 can (about 1 lb) white cannellini beans, drained and rinsed
¾ cup Parmesan cheese, grated

1 Heat the olive oil in a large saucepan, add the bacon and cook gently for 2-3 minutes, stirring all the time to prevent it sticking or burning.
2 Add the parsley and garlic and cook for 2-3 minutes more, stirring all the time.
3 Add all the vegetables except the tomatoes and the canned beans and cook for 4-5 minutes more, continuing to stir all the time, so that the vegetables do not stick.

4 Add the tomatoes with their juice and the broth and bring to a boil. Lower the heat and add salt and pepper to taste. Cover and simmer very gently for about 1½ hours, stirring occasionally.
5 Bring the soup back to a boil, add the pasta, and bring back to a boil again. Simmer for about 15 minutes or until the pasta is almost cooked, that is, it is still firm when tested between thumb and forefinger.
6 Add the beans and continue to cook for a few minutes until the pasta is tender. Taste and adjust seasoning.
7 Allow the soup to stand for 10-15 minutes for the flavor to develop, then ladle into warmed soup bowls. Serve with grated Parmesan cheese passed separately in a small bowl.

Frankfurter and vegetable soup

SERVES 6

¼ lb frankfurters, cut into ¼-inch slices
2 tablespoons vegetable oil
1 cup diced carrots
1 celery stalk, thinly sliced
1½ cups diced turnips
1 onion, chopped
1 clove garlic, crushed (optional)
3 cups beef broth
1 can (about 1 lb) chopped tomatoes
salt and freshly ground black pepper
1 cup shredded green cabbage leaves
¼ cup pasta (see Buying guide)
½ cup grated Cheddar cheese

1 Heat the oil in a heavy-bottomed saucepan, add the carrots, celery, turnips, onion and garlic, if using, and cook over moderate heat for 7 minutes, stirring.

2 Remove from the heat and stir in the broth and tomatoes with their juice. Season to taste with salt and pepper.

3 Return the pan to the heat and bring to a boil. Lower the heat, cover the pan and simmer for 20 minutes.

4 Add the cabbage and pasta, then cover again and simmer for 10 minutes more until the pasta is soft.

5 Stir in the frankfurters, taste and adjust seasoning, and cook for a further 3 minutes.

6 Spoon into warmed individual bowls or a soup tureen and serve at once. Pass the grated cheese in a separate bowl for sprinkling on top of the soup.

Cook's Notes

 TIME
Preparation takes 20 minutes, cooking 45 minutes approximately.

 BUYING GUIDE
If you cannot find soup pasta or pastina, easily, use small pasta shapes or quick-cook pasta broken into ½ in lengths. Cook for 5 minutes, then drain before adding to soup at stage 4.

 VARIATION
Use potatoes or rutabaga in place of turnips.

 FREEZING
Transfer to a rigid container, cool quickly, then seal, label and freeze for up to 6 months. To serve: thaw at room temperature for 2-3 hours, then reheat until bubbling. Add a little more broth if necessary.

 SERVING IDEAS
Serve this hearty soup with toast or whole-wheat bread and follow with a light main course.

●250 calories per portion

Chinese leafy soup

SERVES 4
4 cups chicken broth
1 bunch scallions, finely shredded diagonally including the green tops
1 teaspoon finely grated fresh gingerroot (see Buying guide)
2 teaspoons lemon juice
2 teaspoons soy sauce
salt and freshly ground black pepper
½ cup Chinese fine egg noodles
2-3 lettuce leaves, finely shredded
½ bunch watercress, divided into small sprigs and chopped

1 Heat the broth until on the point of boiling, then add just over half of the scallions together with the grated gingerroot, lemon juice and soy sauce. Half cover with a lid and simmer gently for 5 minutes.

2 Meanwhile, bring a pan of salted water to a boil and cook the egg noodles for 6 minutes until tender.
3 Add the lettuce and watercress to the chicken broth and simmer for 5 minutes more. Adjust seasoning, if necessary, transfer to a warmed serving bowl and garnish with the remaining scallions.
4 Drain the noodles thoroughly, then divide equally between 4 warmed individual soup bowls. Spoon the soup into the bowls of noodles and serve at once.

Cook's Notes

TIME
This soup takes only 30 minutes to make.

SERVING IDEAS
Serve as an appetizer for a Chinese-type meal or as a low-calorie snack with crispbreads or Melba toast.

VARIATIONS
Add a little chopped, cooked chicken or a few chopped, peeled shrimp a few minutes just before the end of cooking time.

ECONOMY
This is an ideal soup for leftovers: use lettuce leaves and sprigs of watercress from a salad and broth made from a chicken carcass.

BUYING GUIDE
Fresh or 'green' ginger is the root of the ginger plant; it is now widely available in supermarkets, as well as the more specialized Chinese food stores. Peel before grating.

●70 calories per portion

Carrot soup with egg and rice

SERVES 4

1½ lb new carrots, thinly sliced
2 tablespoons butter or margarine
2½ cups chicken broth
1 teaspoon sugar
salt and freshly ground black pepper
½ cup milk
⅓ cup cooked rice (see Cook's tips)
4 eggs at room temperature (see Cook's tips)
2 scallions, finely chopped
1 cup thin cream

1 Melt the butter in a saucepan, add the carrots and sauté gently for 2-3 minutes to soften slightly. Stir them to prevent sticking.

2 Add the chicken broth and sugar and season to taste with salt and pepper. Bring to a boil, then lower the heat and simmer, uncovered, for 30 minutes or until the carrots are very tender.

3 Remove the pan from the heat and allow mixture to cool slightly, then pour it into the goblet of a blender and work for a few seconds until smooth. Return the purée to the rinsed-out pan and stir in the milk and the cooked rice. Taste and adjust the seasoning, if necessary.

4 Heat the soup gently until hot but not boiling, then break in the eggs and poach them for about 8 minutes or until they are firm enough to be lifted out with a slotted spoon.

5 Spoon an egg into each of 4 warmed soup bowls and pour over the soup. Sprinkle over the scallions, swirl in the cream and serve the soup at once.

Cook's Notes

 TIME
Preparation takes 15 minutes, cooking takes about 50 minutes.

 SERVING IDEAS
This is a fairly substantial soup, so serve with a light accompaniment such as Melba toast or a selection of crackers, rather than bread roll.

 COOK'S TIPS
If cooking raw rice for this dish, you will need 2 tablespoons to provide ⅓ cup of cooked rice.

Remove the eggs from the refrigerator 1 hour before using: cold eggs will require a longer time to set.

●155 calories per portion

Tomato rice soup

SERVES 4
1 lb fresh tomatoes, chopped
1 can (about 1 lb) tomatoes
1 tablespoon tomato paste
¾ cup water
salt and freshly ground black
    pepper
¼ cup long-grain rice
2 tablespoons medium sherry
    (optional, see Variation)
1 tablespoon finely chopped
    parsley, for garnish

1 Put all the ingredients except the rice, sherry, if using, and parsley into a large saucepan. Bring to a boil, stirring, then lower the heat, cover and simmer for 30 minutes.
2 Push the contents of the saucepan through a strainer, or leave to cool slightly, then purée in a blender and strain (see Cook's tip).
3 Pour the strained tomato purée back into the rinsed-out pan and bring back to the boil. Stir in the rice lower the heat, cover and simmer for about 15 minutes or until the rice is tender.
4 Stir in the sherry, if using, taste and adjust seasoning, then pour into warmed individual soup bowls. Sprinkle with parsley and serve at once.

Cook's Notes

TIME
Preparation and cooking take about 1 hour.

VARIATION
Use 2 tablespoons thin cream instead of sherry, and swirl a little into each bowl before sprinkling with parsley.

SERVING IDEAS
Serve with hot whole-wheat rolls.

COOK'S TIP
It is essential to strain the tomato mixture, to remove the seeds and skins.

●80 calories per portion

Spaghetti with anchovy sauce

SERVES 8
1 lb spaghetti
salt
1 teaspoon vegetable oil
2 tablespoons butter

ANCHOVY SAUCE
2 tablespoons vegetable oil
1 clove garlic, crushed (optional)
1 large onion, finely chopped
1 can (about 2oz) anchovy fillets in oil, mashed to a paste
2 teaspoons all-purpose flour
1 can (about 1 lb) chopped tomatoes
2 teaspoons tomato paste
2 teaspoons dried basil
freshly ground black pepper

1 Bring a large pan of salted water to a boil, swirl in the oil and add the spaghetti. Bring back to a boil then lower the heat and simmer for 10-12 minutes or until the spaghetti is quite tender yet firm to the bite.

2 Meanwhile, make anchovy sauce: heat the oil in a heavy-based skillet, add the garlic, if using, and onion and sauté very gently for 7 minutes until golden.
3 Stir the anchovy paste and flour into the onion and cook, stirring, for 2 minutes more. Gradually blend in the chopped tomatoes and their juices, the tomato paste and basil. Add pepper to taste and simmer gently for 8-10 minutes, stirring occasionally.
4 Drain the pasta thoroughly, then return to the rinsed-out pan. Add the butter and season well with pepper. Toss over low heat until spaghetti is coated in butter.
5 Transfer the spaghetti to warmed serving plates and top with the anchovy sauce. Serve at once. For a finishing touch, see Serving ideas.

Cook's Notes

 TIME
Preparing and cooking the dish take less than 30 minutes in all.

 **WATCHPOINT**
The anchovies are so salty it is wise not to use any salt when seasoning both the sauce and the spaghetti.

 SERVING IDEAS
Sprinkle the top of each platter liberally with finely grated Parmesan cheese to give a true Italian flavour.

 VARIATIONS
For a supper dish rather than a starter, drain a can of tuna and flake into the sauce during cooking. Omit the anchovy if you prefer. Chopped dill pickle, drained capers or chopped, pitted olives may also be added.

●635 calories per portion

Spaghetti supreme

SERVES 6
½ lb wholemeal spaghetti
salt
1 teaspoon vegetable oil
¼ cup butter or margarine
½ lb blue Stilton cheese, cut into
    small cubes
¼ cup walnut pieces, roughly
    chopped
½ cup thin cream
freshly ground black pepper
1 cup finely chopped watercress

1 Bring a large saucepan of salted water to a boil. Swirl in the oil, then add the spaghetti. Bring back to a boil and simmer for about 20 minutes, until the spaghetti is tender but still firm to the bite.
2 Meanwhile, melt the butter in a small saucepan. Add the Stilton and cook over very low heat, mashing with a wooden spoon, until the cheese has melted. Remove the pan from the heat and then stir in the chopped walnuts. Gradually add the cream, stirring vigorously. Season with a little salt and plenty of pepper. Set aside until just before the spaghetti is ready to serve.

3 Return the sauce to low heat, add the watercress and warm through stirring all the time.
4 Drain the spaghetti and rinse with boiling water. Drain again and transfer to a warmed serving dish. Pour over the sauce and then toss gently until the spaghetti is evenly coated with sauce. Serve the dish at once.

Cook's Notes

 TIME
Preparation takes about 30 minutes

WATCHPOINT
Warm the cheese sauce through gently – it will separate if it becomes too hot. If this does happen, remove pan from heat and beat the sauce thoroughly until it is thick, smooth and creamy.

 VARIATION
Try other shapes of wholemeal pasta, such as macaroni or shells or tagliatelle.

 SERVING IDEAS
This is quite a rich and filling appetizer so follow it with a light main course.

●625 calories per portion

Roman salad

SERVES 6
½ lb green tagliatelle (see
   Variation)
salt
1 teaspoon vegetable oil
1 can (about ½ lb) tuna in oil,
   drained, flaked and oil reserved
4 hard-cooked eggs, chopped
2 tomatoes, peeled and chopped
1 can (about 2 oz) anchovy fillets,
   drained, soaked in milk for 20
   minutes, drained and chopped
4 celery stalks, chopped

HERB DRESSING
3 tablespoons vegetable oil
1 tablespoon white wine vinegar
1 teaspoon lemon juice
1 clove garlic, crushed (optional)
pinch of sugar
1 teaspoon finely chopped fresh
   basil
1 tablespoon finely chopped
   parsley
freshly ground black pepper

1 Bring a large pan of salted water to a boil, swirl in the oil and add the tagliatelle. Bring back to a boil and cook for 7-10 minutes (or according to package instructions), until tender yet firm to the bite.
2 Meanwhile, make herb dressing: put the reserved oil from the can of tuna into a screw-top jar with the rest of the dressing ingredients, adding salt and pepper to taste. Replace the lid firmly and shake the jar thoroughly until dressing is completely blended.
3 Drain the pasta, rinse under cold running water and drain again thoroughly.
4 Put the cooked pasta in a salad bowl. Add the tuna, chopped hard-cooked eggs, tomatoes, anchovies and celery. Pour over the herb dressing and toss the ingredients lightly together: Serve at once (see Serving ideas).

Cook's Notes

TIME
This tasty salad only takes about 20 minutes to prepare.

WATCHPOINT
Rinsing pasta is necessary to remove excess starch, thus preventing the noodles sticking together.

SERVING IDEAS
This makes 6 individual helpings for a dinner-party starter. For a more substantial salad, garnish with chopped green pepper, tomato quarters, halved and pitted ripe olives or preserved walnuts, and a few celery leaves. Serve with hot rolls and butter.

VARIATION
This salad can be made using any of the many varieties of large pasta shapes available such as pasta shells, bows or wheels.

●580 calories per portion

Tagliatelle in parsley sauce

SERVES 6
¾ lb fresh tagliatelle (see Buying guide)
1 tablespoon vegetable oil
grated Parmesan cheese, to serve

SAUCE
1 cup fresh parsley sprigs
2 large cloves garlic, chopped
2 tablespoons pignoli (see Buying guide)
½ cup olive oil (see Economy)
salt
½ cup grated Parmesan cheese
freshly ground black pepper

1 First make the sauce: put the parsley, garlic, pignoli and oil into a blender (see Cook's tips). Add pinch of salt and purée for 1 minute. Add all of the grated Parmesan cheese and purée for 1 minute more, then season with pepper to taste. It should be spicy.

2 Bring a large pan of salted water to a boil. Add the oil and tagliatelle and stir once. Bring back to a boil and cook for 2-3 minutes until *al dente* (tender, yet firm to the bite).

3 Drain the tagliatelle well, then turn into a warmed serving dish. Stir the sauce and add to the dish. Quickly toss the tagliatelle with 2 forks to mix it with the sauce. Serve at once while still hot, with a bowl filled with grated Parmesan cheese passed separately.

Cook's Notes

TIME
Preparation and cooking take about 30 minutes.

ECONOMY
Use half olive and half vegetable oil.

COOK'S TIPS
If you do not have a blender, pound the garlic, nuts and salt to a paste in a mortar, then slowly work in the parsley, cheese and oil.

Store the sauce in a covered container in the refrigerator for a few days. Bring to room temperature before using.

BUYING GUIDE
Remember you can buy fresh tagliatelle (or egg noodles) from Italian delicatessens and some supermarkets. If fresh tagliatelle is unavailable you can use the dried type and cook according to package instructions.

Pignoli, sold in health food stores, are small tapering nuts with a soft, oily texture and resinous flavor. Alternatively, you can use unsalted cashew nuts if you prefer a milder taste.

●735 calories per portion

17

Mushroom and ham medley

SERVES 6
½ lb button mushrooms, chopped
  (see Buying guide)
salt
1 teaspoon vegetable oil
¼ cup pasta shells or bows
1¼ cups chicken broth
2 tablespoons butter or margarine
¼ cup all-purpose flour
1¼ cups milk
1 can (¾ lb) whole corn kernels,
  drained
¼ lb diced cooked ham
freshly ground black pepper
2 tablespoons chopped fresh
  parsley, for garnish

1 Bring a large pan of salted water to a boil, swirl in the oil, then add the pasta. Bring back to a boil and cook for 7-10 minutes until tender but firm to the bite.

2 Meanwhile, in a separate large saucepan, heat the broth with the butter or margarine until boiling. Add the mushrooms, lower the heat and simmer for up to 5 minutes until the mushrooms are soft.

3 Put the flour in a bowl, then gradually beat in the milk with a wire whisk. Stir the milk and flour mixture into the mushrooms in the saucepan, bring to a boil, then lower the heat and simmer for a few minutes, stirring.

4 Drain the pasta and stir into the mushroom mixture with the corn and ham. Season to taste with salt and pepper and heat through very gently, stirring occasionally.

5 Pour into warmed soup bowls and sprinkle with parsley.

Cook's Notes

 TIME
Preparation and cooking the soup take about 25 minutes in all.

 SERVING IDEAS
This dish is best eaten like a thick soup, with a spoon. Serve with peda or French bread, plain or toasted, spread with butter, if liked.

 BUYING GUIDE
Flat mushrooms can be used in place of button mushrooms. They will give a stronger, more distinctive flavor, but they may make the dish rather darker in color.

●230 calories per portion.

18

Savory pasta

SERVES 6-8
2 cups pasta shapes
salt
few drops of vegetable oil
¼ cup bacon slices, finely chopped
1 large onion, thinly sliced
3 tablespoons all-purpose flour
1 teaspoon dry mustard
2 cups warm milk
4 sage leaves, chopped, or
    1 teaspoon dried sage
3 tablespoons chopped parsley
freshly ground black pepper
3 egg yolks
2 cups grated Cheddar cheese
2 tablespoons wheatgerm (see
    Buying guide)

1 Preheat oven to 400°.
2 Bring a large saucepan of salted water to a boil, add the oil, then add the pasta and stir well. Bring back to a boil, lower the heat and cook for about 10 minutes until the pasta is *al dente* (see page 4).
3 Meanwhile, put the bacon in a large saucepan, place over low heat and cook until the fat begins to run. Add the onion, raise the heat and cook until the onion is softened.
4 Sprinkle in the flour and dry mustard, then stir over low heat for 2 minutes. Remove from the heat and gradually stir in the milk. Return to the heat and simmer, stirring, until thick and smooth. Add the herbs then season to taste.
5 Remove the pan from the heat and beat in the egg yolks one at a time. Drain the pasta and stir into the sauce with two-thirds of the grated cheese.
6 Pile the mixture into a large flameproof dish and smooth the top. Cover with the remaining cheese and sprinkle the wheatgerm over the top.
7 Bake in the oven for 25 minutes, then place under a heated broiler for a few minutes to brown the top. Serve at once.

Cook's Notes

TIME
This dish can be prepared and cooked in just under 1 hour.

VARIATIONS
Wholemeal pasta shapes may be used instead of plain pasta.
    The bacon may be omitted and 2 tablespoons margarine used for cooking the onion.

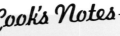

BUYING GUIDE
It is worth buying wheatgerm specially for this dish, as it not only gives a good texture to the topping but is also an excellent source of proteins, fats and vitamins D and E. Wheatgerm is available from health food shops, but if you cannot obtain it, use the same quantity of wholewheat bread crumbs instead.

COOK'S TIPS
If you are careful to mix the pasta and sauce together quickly while they are both still hot, then there is no need to bake this dish in the oven to heat through. It will be hot enough if just put under the broiler until the top is golden brown.

●455 calories per portion

19

Salami shell salad

SERVES 6-8
2 cups pasta wheels or shells
salt
1 teaspoon vegetable oil
6 oz salami, cut into strips 1½ inches long and ½-inch wide
8 scallions, each cut into 4 lengths
1 can (about 14 oz) artichoke hearts, drained, rinsed and halved (see Variations)
½ cup ripe olives
2 tomatoes, each cut into 8 wedges
lettuce leaves, to serve

DRESSING
3 tablespoons vegetable oil
1 tablespoon white wine vinegar
½ teaspoon sugar
½ teaspoon dry mustard
freshly ground black pepper

1 Bring a large pan of salted water to a boil, swirl in the oil and add the pasta. Cook for 7-10 minutes or until tender yet firm. Rinse under cold running water and drain.
2 Put the pasta wheels in a large bowl and mix the salami, scallions, artichoke halves, ripe olives and tomato wedges.
3 Make the dressing: put all the ingredients in a screw-top jar, adding salt and pepper to taste, and shake well to mix.
4 Pour the dressing over the pasta mixture and toss until coated and all the ingredients are well mixed.
5 Arrange lettuce leaves around the edge of a serving dish, then spoon the pasta mixture into the center.

Cook's Notes

 TIME
Cooking the pasta wheels and preparing the salad take 20 minutes.

●565 calories per portion

 VARIATIONS
Use drained canned asparagus instead of artichoke hearts.

Add chopped fresh herbs, such as coriander or tarragon, crumbled Feta cheese or 1 tablespoon tomato paste to vary the flavor. To turn this into a main-course for 4 add sliced button mushrooms and cooked whole green beans.

20

Pasta with peppers

SERVES 4
1½ cups pasta bows
1 small red pepper, seeded
1 small green pepper, seeded
3 tablespoons olive oil
1 small onion, finely chopped
1 garlic clove, crushed (optional)
1 teaspoon dried oregano
1 cup ripe olives
salt and ground black pepper

1 Cut the red and green peppers into thin 2-inch lengths.

2 Heat the oil in a large saucepan, add the onion and garlic, if using, and sauté gently for 5 minutes until soft and lightly colored.

3 Add the peppers, oregano, salt and pepper and cook for 10 minutes more, stirring from time to time.

4 Meanwhile, bring a large pan of salted water to a boil. Add the pasta and bring back to a boil, then lower the heat and simmer for about 10 minutes or until the pasta is just tender. Drain thoroughly.

5 Add the pasta and olives to the onion and peppers and mix well. Cook over low heat for 2 minutes more, stirring occasionally. Transfer to a warmed serving dish.

Cook's Notes

 TIME
Preparation and cooking take about 30 minutes.

 COOK'S TIP
Make sure the pasta bows are drained well; if the water is left inside them the finished dish will be soggy and unappetizing.

 VARIATIONS
The peppers and olives go very well with many other types of pasta. The dish can also be served cold as a salad to accompany a meat dish or as part of a buffet.

● 270 calories per portion

Salmon kedgeree

SERVES 6
2 cans (7 oz each) red salmon,
drained and flaked
¾ cup long-grain rice
salt
3 hard-cooked eggs
¼ cup butter
freshly ground black pepper
½ cup dairy sour cream or yogurt
2 teaspoons curry powder
paprika, for garnish

1 Cook the rice in plenty of boiling salted water until tender but not mushy (about 12 minutes). Drain in a strainer and rinse thoroughly, first under cold water, then hot.
2 Place the rice in a warmed, buttered shallow serving dish, cover and keep warm in a low oven.
3 Chop 1 of the hard-cooked eggs and the white of the others, reserving the yolks.

4 Melt the butter in a saucepan over moderate heat. Add the salmon and the chopped egg, then shake the pan briefly over the heat to warm through. Season with salt and pepper. Add the salmon and egg to the rice.
5 In a small saucepan, warm through the dairy sour cream or yogurt over low heat, but do not allow to boil. Stir in the curry powder, beat until smooth, then pour over the rice mixture and fork through lightly.
6 Press the reserved egg yolks through a strainer over the top of the kedgeree. Sprinkle with paprika to taste and serve at once.

Cook's Notes

 TIME
This dish takes 25 minutes to make.

 SERVING IDEAS
Serve with mango chutney. For a supper dish, serve with a green salad and ½ cucumber, thinly sliced and mixed with plain yogurt.

 **COOK'S TIPS**
When rinsing the rice, make a few holes in it with a spoon handle to drain it well and prevent it sticking.

Instead of keeping rice hot in the oven, an alternative way is to put the rice in a strainer over a pan of hot water and cover with a clean, folded dish-towel.

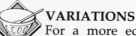 **VARIATIONS**
For a more economical dish, use canned tuna in place of salmon. For a traditional kedgeree, use 1 lb finnan haddie poached in milk to cover, with a bay leaf and a few black peppercorns added.

●465 calories per portion

Stuffed cabbage leaves

SERVES 6
12 large cabbage leaves
salt
1 tablespoon vegetable oil
1 small onion, finely chopped
4 bacon slices, chopped
1 cup cooked rice (see Cook's tips)
½ cup cream cheese
2 tablespoons half-and-half
3 tomatoes, peeled and chopped
½ cup chopped mixed nuts
2 teaspoons paprika
freshly ground black pepper
¼ cup chicken broth
margarine, for greasing

1 Preheat oven to 350° and grease a large flameproof dish with margarine (see Cook's tips).
2 Bring a pan of salted water to a boil. Discard the tough rib at the base of the cabbage leaves and blanch them in the boiling water for 3 minutes. Drain carefully, refresh under cold running water, lay flat on a work surface and pat dry with kitchen paper.
3 Heat the oil in a small skillet, add the onion and bacon and sauté gently for 5 minutes until the onion is limp and lightly colored.
4 Using a slotted spoon, transfer the onion and bacon to a bowl and add the rice, cheese, milk, tomatoes, nuts and paprika. Mix ingredients together thoroughly. Season to taste with salt and black pepper.
5 Divide the mixture between the cabbage leaves, putting it in the center of each leaf. Fold the 2 sides over the filling and then roll up each leaf to form a neat parcel.
6 Place the parcels, join side down, in the prepared dish. Season lightly with salt and pepper, then pour the chicken broth over the parcels. Cover and bake in the oven for 1 hour. Serve at once.

Cook's Notes

 TIME
Preparation takes about 30 minutes, and the cooking takes 1 hour.

 BUYING GUIDE
Any type of cabbage is suitable – Savoy or red or white cabbage is ideal.

 SPECIAL OCCASION
Substitute white or red wine for the chicken broth to add extra flavor.

 SERVING IDEAS
This could also be served as an accompaniment to meat dishes.

 COOK'S TIPS
You will need to cook ⅓ cup raw rice to get 1 cup cooked rice.
Choose a flameproof dish large enough to accommodate the rolls in a single layer.

●530 calories per portion

Mixed fruit curry

SERVES 4

¼ cup creamed coconut, broken into pieces (see Buying guide)
2 tablespoons curry paste (see Cook's tips)
½ cup dairy sour cream
1 banana
½ honeydew melon, cut into 1-inch cubes (see Buying guide)
1 cup each green and black grapes, halved and seeded
1 orange, divided into sections
1 red dessert apple, cored (see Cook's tips)

1 Put the coconut, curry paste and sour cream into a large saucepan. Stir over low heat until the mixture is well blended and warmed through. Do not let boil.

2 Peel the banana, cut into ½-inch slices and add to pan with the melon, grapes and orange. Cook gently, stirring, for 3-4 minutes un-til the fruit is warm. Cut the apple into wedges, stir in and warm through. Spoon into a serving dish and serve at once.

Cook's Notes

TIME
20 minutes preparation, 5-6 minutes cooking.

SERVING IDEAS
Serve as a hot, refreshing appetizer on a bed of plain boiled rice. The rice should be cooked *al dente* and with each grain separate.

BUYING GUIDE
Blocks of creamed coconut are available in packages from supermarkets and Indian food stores.
Choose a melon that is not too ripe or it will break up.

VARIATIONS
Add ¾ cup diced cooked chicken, ham or bacon to the fruit mixture to make a more substantial dish.

COOK'S TIPS
Use an apple corer to remove the core and leave the peel on to add color.
Use curry paste for this dish rather than curry powder. As the dish is only cooked for a few minutes, curry powder will give an uncooked flavor.

●280 calories per portion

24

Risotto alla Milanese

SERVES 6
¼ cup butter
1 onion, very finely chopped
1½ cups Italian rice (see Buying guide)
¼ cup dry white wine
5 cups hot chicken broth
¼ teaspoon powdered saffron (optional)
2 tablespoons finely grated Parmesan cheese
salt and freshly ground black pepper
extra Parmesan cheese, to serve

1 Melt half the butter in a heavy-bottomed saucepan, add the onion and sauté gently for 5 minutes until limp and lightly colored.
2 Add the rice and continue to cook for 3 minutes more, stirring con-

Cook's Notes

TIME
Preparation and cooking take 20-25 minutes.

WATCHPOINT
Take care not to 'mash' the rice at stage 6.

BUYING GUIDE
Choose a medium-grain Italian rice rather than the more usual long-grain type. Arborio is ideal and can be found at Italian delicatessen stores.

SERVING IDEAS
Besides serving as an unusual appetizer, *Risotto alla Milanese* is the traditional accompaniment to the veal dish, *Osso buco*. It is delicious served with any meat casserole or stew.

●455 calories per portion

stantly with a wooden spoon.
3 Add the wine and cook for 2 minutes more, stirring.
4 Stir in hot broth, about a cup at a time, adding more as soon as each addition has been absorbed. If using saffron, dissolve the powder in 2 tablespoons of hot broth and add with the last addition. When all the broth has been absorbed, the rice should be moist and just creamy.
5 When the grains of rice are tender but still firm, remove from the heat, add the remaining butter and sprinkle with the Parmesan cheese. Cover with a lid and leave to stand for 2 minutes.
6 Season well with salt and pepper and mix thoroughly with a fork. Top with extra Parmesan cheese.

EVERYDAY MAIN COURSES

Cannelloni with tuna

SERVES 4
12 cannelloni tubes (see Buying guide)
¼ cup butter or margarine
½ cup all-purpose flour
2¼ cups milk
1 can (about 7 oz) tuna, drained and flaked
1 cup frozen petits pois (see Buying guide)
salt and freshly ground black pepper
1 tablespoon tomato paste
generous pinch of paprika
½ cup grated sharp Cheddar cheese
2 tablespoons grated Parmesan cheese
margarine or butter, for greasing

1 Preheat oven to 400°. Grease a shallow flameproof dish.
2 Make the filling: melt the butter in a saucepan, sprinkle in the flour and stir over low heat for 1-2 minutes until straw-colored. Remove from the heat and gradually stir in 1¼ cups of the milk. Return to the heat and simmer, stirring, until the sauce is thick and smooth. Remove from the heat.
3 Spoon half this sauce into a bowl, then fold in the tuna and peas with salt and pepper to taste.
4 With a small teaspoon, or a forcing bag fitted with a large plain nozzle, fill the cannelloni with the filling mixture, pushing it well into the tubes.
5 Over low heat, gradually stir the remaining milk into the reserved sauce in the pan. Beat vigorously until smooth, then add the tomato paste, paprika and salt and pepper to taste, then simmer for a few minutes until thickened.
6 Cover the bottom of the prepared dish with a little of the hot sauce, then arrange the cannelloni on top, separating each one with a little sauce. Cover with the remaining sauce. Mix the cheeses together,

then sprinkle over the top.
7 Bake in the oven for 30-35 minutes until the sauce is bubbling at the edges and the cannelloni are cooked through. Serve hot, straight from the dish.

Cook's Notes

 TIME
Preparation takes 40 minutes, baking about 30-35 minutes.

 VARIATION
Use 1 cup cooked ham or Italian salami, finely chopped, instead of the tuna.

 BUYING GUIDE
Be sure to buy cannelloni that do not need pre-cooking. This is stated on the package.
Petits pois are the smallest variety of frozen peas available, and the most suitable for filling cannelloni. If difficult to obtain, use ordinary frozen peas.

 DID YOU KNOW
Cannelloni is a favorite dish in Italy; the filling often includes veal, ham, curd cheese or spinach.

 SERVING IDEAS
Serve the cannelloni with a mixed salad.

●530 calories per portion

Beef and spinach savory

SERVES 4
1 lb lean ground beef
1 tablespoon butter or margarine
1 tablespoon vegetable oil
1 large onion, chopped
4 tomatoes, chopped
1 tablespoon tomato paste
1 tablespoon mushroom catsup
salt and freshly ground black
  pepper
¼ lb vermicelli (see Buying guide)
1 lb frozen chopped spinach
1 large egg
1 tablespoon grated Parmesan
  cheese
½ teaspoon freshly grated nutmeg
½ cup dairy cream
¼ lb mushrooms, sliced
2 large tomatoes, sliced
1 cup grated Cheddar cheese
margarine, for greasing

1 Heat the butter and oil in a large saucepan, add the onion and sauté gently for 5 minutes, until limp and lightly colored. Add the ground beef, turn the heat to high and cook for 5 minutes more or until the meat has lost all its pinkness. Keep stirring with a wooden spoon to prevent the meat from sticking.

2 Add the tomatoes with their juice, tomato paste and mushroom catsup. Stir well, bring to a boil and season with salt and pepper. Lower the heat, cover and simmer for about 30 minutes.

3 Meanwhile, bring a large saucepan of salted water to a boil, add the vermicelli and cook for about 5 minutes, until just tender. Cook the chopped spinach according to package instructions.

4 Preheat oven to 350°. Grease a shallow flameproof dish.

5 Drain the vermicelli and cut it up roughly (see Preparation). Beat the egg and Parmesan cheese together in a bowl, and season with pepper and nutmeg. Add the chopped vermicelli and fork it through well. Spoon over base of dish.

6 Drain the spinach and put it into a bowl. Stir in the sour cream.

7 Spoon the beef and tomato mixture over the vermicelli. Arrange the sliced mushrooms on top and evenly spoon over the spinach and cream mixture.

8 Top with the tomato slices and sprinkle with the grated cheese. Cook in the oven for 20-30 minutes, until the cheese topping is melted and golden.

Cook's Notes

 TIME
Preparation and cooking this dish take just over 1 hour.

 BUYING GUIDE
Vermicelli, very thin pasta, cooks in half the time taken for spaghetti.

 PREPARATION
To cut up vermicelli:

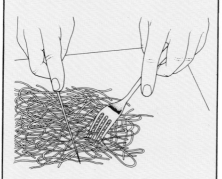

Use a knife and fork to cut up the vermicelli roughly on a wooden chopping board.

●635 calories per portion

Fishy noodle ring

SERVES 4
6 oz ribbon noodles (see Cook's tip)
salt
1 tablespoon vegetable oil
4 eggs, beaten
1¼ cups milk
¼ teaspoon paprika
2 tablespoons butter, melted
watercress sprigs, for garnish

FISH SAUCE
1 lb cod fillets, skinned and cut
    into bite-sized pieces
2 tablespoons vegetable oil
1 large onion, chopped
1½ lb tomatoes, peeled and
    chopped
2 tablespoons tomato paste
2 teaspoons dried basil
½ teaspoon sugar
freshly ground black pepper

1 Preheat oven to 350°.
2 Bring a large saucepan of salted water to a boil. Add the oil, then the noodles. Bring back to a boil, then lower the heat and simmer for 10-12 minutes until the noodles are tender but firm to the bite.
3 Meanwhile, beat the eggs and milk together in a bowl. Add the paprika and pinch of salt.
4 Use half the melted butter to grease a 5 cup ring mold very generously. Stir the remainder of the melted butter into the egg and milk mixture and pour into the buttered ring mold.
5 Drain the noodles, then spoon into the ring mold, arranging them evenly around it. Gently fork them into the liquid. Put the ring mold into a large roasting pan and half fill the pan with boiling water. Cook in oven for 40 minutes or until the mold filling has set.
6 Meanwhile, make the sauce: heat the oil in a saucepan, add the onion and sauté gently for 5 minutes until limp and lightly colored. Add the tomatoes and the paste and cook for about 20 minutes, until the sauce is thick. Stir in the basil and the sugar and then season with salt and pepper to taste.
7 Carefully lower the fish into the pan, stirring to coat the pieces in sauce. Cook for another 5 minutes or until the fish flakes easily when tested with a fork.
8 To serve: run a knife around the edge of the mold, then invert a warmed serving plate on top. Hold the mold and plate firmly together and invert them, giving a sharp shake halfway round. Lift off the mold. Spoon some of the sauce into the middle and garnish with watercress. Spoon remainder of sauce into a warmed serving dish and pass separately.

Cook's Notes

 TIME
Preparation takes about 30 minutes. Cooking time is 40 minutes.

 COOK'S TIP
Use green or white tagliatelle-type noodles, or a mixture of both colors.

 SERVING IDEAS
This makes a satisfying, tasty main-course dish served with a green salad tossed in a generous dressing of well-seasoned oil and vinegar.

 VARIATIONS
The noodle ring may also be served cold: prepare to end of stage 5, then leave to cool completely. Omit stages 6 and 7, then unmold as in stage 8 and fill the ring with cold cooked fish pieces or prawns in a tomato-flavored mayonnaise.

WATCHPOINT
Butter the ring mold generously or the noodle ring will stick.

●530 calories per portion

28

Finnan haddie lasagne

SERVES 4

1½ lb finnan haddie fillets, skinned
2 bay leaves
pinch of ground cloves
1 onion, sliced
1 cup water
½ cup dry white wine
2 tablespoons butter or margarine
2 tablespoons all-purpose flour
1 cup grated Cheddar cheese
freshly ground black pepper
6 tomatoes, peeled and sliced
½ lb lasagne (see Buying guide)
3 tablespoons fresh wholewheat bread crumbs
1 tablespoon snipped chives
salt
margarine, for greasing
few extra bay leaves, for garnish (optional)

1 Preheat oven to 350°. Grease a flameproof dish.

2 Place the finnan haddie in a large skillet and add the bay leaves, cloves and sliced onion. Pour the water and wine over the fish and bring to the boil. Lower the heat and simmer for 10 minutes, or until the fish flesh flakes easily when pierced with a sharp knife or prodded gently with a fork.

3 Using a spatula, transfer the fish to a plate and leave to cool. Strain the cooking liquid into a measuring jug and measure out 1¼ cups. Reserve the onion.

4 Flake the fish, discarding the skin and any bones.

5 Melt the butter in a saucepan. Sprinkle in the flour and stir over low heat for 1-2 minutes, until straw-colored. Gradually stir in the measured cooking liquid, then simmer, stirring, until thick and smooth. Stir all but 2 tablespoons of the cheese into the sauce, then add the flaked fish and reserved onion. Season to taste with pepper.

6 Place one-third of the fish mixture in the prepared dish and arrange half the tomato slices on top. Cover with half the lasagne. Repeat the layers once, then top the dish with the remaining one-third of the fish mixture.

7 Mix together the bread crumbs, remaining grated cheese and the chives in a bowl. Season to taste with salt and pepper and sprinkle the mixture evenly over the fish.

8 Cook in the oven for 30 minutes, until the lasagne is heated through and the topping is golden brown. Garnish with bay leaves, if liked.

Cook's Notes

TIME
Preparation takes about 30 minutes, cooking about 30 minutes.

BUYING GUIDE
Buy the type of lasagne that does not need pre-boiling but just requires heating through in the oven. It is widely available from supermarkets: check the package carefully.

●525 calories per portion

Beef and bean lasagne

SERVES 4

1 lb lean ground beef
2 tablespoons plus 1 teaspoon
  vegetable oil
2 onions, chopped
1 large green pepper, seeded and
  chopped
2 tomatoes, peeled and chopped
1 tablespoon tomato paste
½ teaspoon dried oregano
1 beef bouillon cube, crumbled
½ tablespoon all-purpose flour
salt and freshly ground black
  pepper
7 oz lasagne
1 can (about 1 lb) baked beans
¾ cup grated Cheddar cheese

1 Heat 2 tablespoons oil in a skillet. Add the onions and sauté gently for 3-4 minutes until limp but not colored. Add the green pepper and cook for 2-3 minutes more, then add the ground beef, stirring with a wooden spoon to remove any lumps. Continue cooking for 3-4 minutes, stirring from time to time.

2 Add the tomatoes, tomato paste, oregano, bouillon cube, flour and salt and pepper to taste. Stir well to mix, then continue cooking gently for 20 minutes, stirring occasionally.

3 Meanwhile, add 1 teaspoon oil to a large pan of salted water and bring to a boil. Add the lasagne, a piece at a time (see Cook's tip) and boil rapidly, uncovered, for about 10 minutes or until just tender, stirring frequently. Drain, rinse then drain on kitchen paper.

4 Preheat oven to 400°.

5 Spoon a thin layer of meat sauce into a deep flameproof dish and cover with 2-3 pieces of lasagne. Spoon more of the meat sauce over one half and spoon some of the beans over the other half. Cover with another 2-3 pieces of lasagne. Spoon more meat sauce over the half where the beans were in the previous layer and more beans over the previous meat sauce layer. Continue layering and alternating the meat sauce and beans with the lasagne, ending with a layer of meat sauce and beans.

6 Sprinkle with the grated cheese, then bake in the oven for 20-25 minutes until the cheese is browned and the dish is bubbling.

Cook's Notes

TIME
This substantial supper dish takes about 35 minutes to prepare and 20-25 minutes to cook.

COOK'S TIP
To make it easier to fit the lasagne into the pan, break it into 2-3 pieces before cooking.

SERVING IDEAS
Serve with a lettuce and watercress salad.

●615 calories per portion

Chicken Tetrazzini

SERVES 4
2 cups diced cooked chicken
salt
¼ lb spaghetti
¼ cup butter
¼ lb whole button mushrooms
⅓ cup all-purpose flour
2 cups chicken broth
¼ cup dry white wine
½ cup thick cream
pinch of freshly grated nutmeg
freshly ground black pepper
1oz Parmesan cheese, grated

1 Preheat oven to 350°.
2 Bring a large saucepan of salted water to a boil, add the spaghetti and cook until just tender, 10-12 minutes. Drain well. Return spaghetti to the rinsed-out pan, cover with fresh cold water (see Cook's tip). Set aside.
3 Meanwhile, melt the butter in a saucepan, add the mushrooms and sauté, stirring occasionally, for about 5 minutes until just tender. Remove mushrooms with a slotted spoon and set aside.
4 Sprinkle the flour into the butter

in the pan and stir over low heat for 1-2 minutes. Gradually stir in the broth and simmer, stirring, until the sauce is thickened and smooth. Remove from the heat and gradually stir in the wine and cream. Add the nutmeg and then season to taste with salt and freshly ground black pepper.

5 Drain the spaghetti thoroughly, then stir it into the sauce with the cooked mushrooms and chicken.
6 Pour the mixture into a shallow 5-cup flameproof dish. Sprinkle the grated Parmesan cheese over the top and bake in the oven for about 30 minutes until golden. Serve hot, straight from the dish.

Cook's Notes

 TIME
Preparation takes about 35 minutes, cooking about 30 minutes.

 ECONOMY
The cream and broth may be replaced by a mixture of 1¼ cups milk and 1¼ cups broth. Replace the wine with cider and the Parmesan with ½ cup grated Cheddar cheese.

 COOK'S TIP
The cooked spaghetti must be covered with cold water until it is required, to prevent the strands from sticking together.

●540 calories per portion

FREEZING
Use a rigid foil container but do not sprinkle the dish with the cheese. Cool quickly, then seal, label and freeze for up to 3 months. To serve: reheat from frozen in a 350° oven for about 1 hour. Stir the dish with a fork once or twice during cooking, and sprinkle with the cheese halfway through cooking time.

? DID YOU KNOW
Chicken Tetrazzini is believed to have been created by the chef at Delmonico's, a famous New York restaurant, in honor of one of its best customers, Louisa Tetrazzini, who happened to be extremely fond of spaghetti.

Pasta pie

SERVES 4
¾ lb fresh tagliatelle (see Buying guide)
salt
1 teaspoon vegetable oil
2 tablespoons butter or margarine
1 onion, roughly chopped
1 tablespoon all-purpose flour
1¼ cups milk
1½ cups diced cooked chicken
1 can whole corn kernels, drained
freshly ground black pepper
½ cup grated Cheddar cheese
margarine, for greasing

1 Preheat oven to 400° and lightly grease a 7-cup flameproof dish.
2 Bring a large pan of salted water to a boil, swirl in the oil and add the pasta. Bring back to a boil and then cook for 1 minute only. Drain well and leave to cool.
3 Meanwhile, melt the butter in a saucepan, add the onion and sauté for about 3-4 minutes until limp but not colored. Sprinkle in the flour and stir over low heat for 1-2 minutes until straw-colored. Remove from heat and gradually stir in the

milk. Return to the heat and simmer, stirring, until thick and smooth.
4 Stir in the chicken and corn and season with salt and pepper.
5 Using scissors, cut up the pasta. Use two-thirds to line the prepared

dish (see Preparation).
6 Pour the chicken mixture into the center of the pasta. Place the rest of the pasta over the top. Sprinkle over the grated cheese and bake in the oven for about 25 minutes, until the top is lightly browned.

Cook's Notes

TIME
Preparation, including cooling time, is about 45 minutes. Cooking takes about 25 minutes.

WATCHPOINT
Most pasta recipes advise rinsing pasta under cold running water to remove excess starch. Do not rinse the pasta in this recipe however, as the starch is needed to make it easier to line the prepared dish satisfactorily.

BUYING GUIDE
If fresh tagliatelle is not available, use 6 oz dried tagliatelle and cook for 7-8 minutes in stage 2.

● 630 calories per portion

PREPARATION
To line the dish with tagliatelle:

1 *Using scissors, cut the pasta into pieces the length of the dish.*

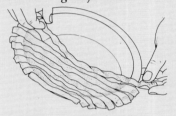

2 *Start at center of dish and lay pasta until the whole dish is covered.*

Pasta with chicken livers

SERVES 2-4

½ lb frozen chicken livers, thawed
  and cut into small pieces (see
  Buying guide)
2 tablespoons margarine
½ onion, thinly sliced
2-4 tablespoons all-purpose flour
¼ cup medium-dry sherry
½ cup mushrooms, sliced
½ cup chicken broth
½ teaspoon dried thyme
salt and freshly ground black
  pepper
¾ lb pasta
1 tablespoon butter
1 tablespoon half-and-half
little grated Parmesan (optional)
fresh thyme sprigs (optional)

1 Melt the margarine in a saucepan, add the onion and sauté gently until limp but not colored.
2 Toss the chicken livers in the flour to coat them. Add the chicken livers to the pan, raise the heat slightly and cook for 3-4 minutes until browned but still pink inside.
3 Add the sherry to the pan, then stir in the mushrooms. Stir in the chicken broth and bring to a boil. Add the thyme and season to taste with salt and pepper. Lower the heat, cover the pan and simmer gently for 12 minutes.
4 Meanwhile, cook the pasta according to package directions until tender. Drain the cooked pasta and return to the rinsed-out pan with the butter and pepper to taste. Shake the pan vigorously to coat the pasta in the butter and pepper.
5 To serve: stir the half-and-half into the chicken liver sauce. Transfer the pasta to a warmed serving dish and spoon over the chicken liver sauce. Top with the Parmesan and thyme, if using. Serve at once.

Cook's Notes

 TIME
Preparation and cooking the sauce and pasta take 40 minutes.

 FREEZING
To freeze the chicken liver sauce, cool thoroughly then freeze in a polythene bag for up to 6 weeks. Thaw at room temperature before gently heating through to serve.

BUYING GUIDE
Frozen chicken livers are usually sold in plastic cartons and are ready for cooking. They are available from most supermarkets. Fresh chicken livers can be used; many butchers supply them. Take care to remove any trace of green sac which will make the liver taste very bitter.

●525 calories per portion

33

Macaroni turkey

SERVES 4

1½ lb boneless turkey meat, cut into 1-inch cubes (see Buying guide)
1 tablespoon vegetable oil
¼ cup butter or margarine
1 large onion, chopped
2 celery stalks, chopped
2 teaspoons all-purpose flour
1 can (about 10 oz) condensed cream of chicken soup
1¼ cups chicken broth
salt and ground black pepper
2 teaspoons Dijon-style mustard
1½ cups wholemeal macaroni
½ lb mushrooms, sliced
2 tablespoons chopped parsley
1 cup fresh white bread crumbs
tomato slices, for garnish

1 Heat oil and half the butter in a large skillet. Add the onion and celery and sauté gently for 1-2 minutes. Add the turkey and sauté briskly for 3-4 minutes more, stirring often, to brown on all sides.
2 Sprinkle the flour into the skillet and stir over low heat for 1-2 minutes. Remove from the heat and stir in the soup and the chicken broth. Return to heat and bring to a boil, stirring. Season to taste. Lower the heat, add the mustard and simmer for 20 minutes.
3 Preheat oven to 400°.
4 Bring a large pan of salted water to a boil and cook the macaroni for 10 minutes. Drain well. Melt the remaining butter in the rinsed-out pan, add the macaroni and stir it well to coat thoroughly.
5 Spoon the macaroni over the bottom of a large flameproof dish.
6 Stir the sliced mushrooms into the turkey mixture and spoon evenly over macaroni. Sprinkle with the parsley and bread crumbs and bake for 20 minutes to brown. Serve hot, straight from the dish, garnished with tomato slices.

Spicy sausage macaroni

SERVES 4-6

1 lb chorizo sausages (see Buying
   guide)
salt
¾ lb elbow macaroni
1 tablespoon shortening
1 small onion, finely chopped
2 cans (9 oz each) tomato or
   mushroom spaghetti sauce
1 teaspoon dried oregano (optional)
freshly ground black pepper
1½ cups grated mild Cheddar
   cheese
margarine, for greasing

1 Bring a large saucepan of salted
water to a boil. Meanwhile, remove
skin from the sausages.

2 Preheat oven to 350°. Drop the
macaroni into the boiling water and
cook according to instructions until
just tender. Drain thoroughly.

3 While the macaroni is cooking,
melt the lard in a large skillet, add
the sausages and cook, turning,
until brown on all sides. Remove
the sausages from the pan, drain on
absorbent paper and set aside.

4 Add the onion to the pan and
sauté gently, stirring often, until it
is limp and golden. Remove from
the pan with a slotted spoon and
pour away the fat left in the pan.

5 Cut the sausages into ½-inch
pieces. Return to the pan with the
onion, spaghetti sauce and oregano,
if using. Season carefully with salt
and pepper. Bring the contents of
the pan to simmering point.

6 Lightly grease a 1½ quart casserole. Form separate layers of macaroni, sausage and sauce, and one-
third of the cheese. Repeat these
layers once, then finish with a layer
of macaroni. Sprinkle the top with
the remaining one-third of the
grated cheese, making sure all the
macaroni is covered.

7 Bake in the oven for about 30
minutes, until the topping is golden
and the macaroni heated through.
Serve at once.

Cook's Notes

TIME
Preparation, including
boiling the pasta, takes
about 20 minutes. Cooking in
the oven takes about 30 minutes.

BUYING GUIDE
Chorizos are sold
cooked and uncooked in
delicatessens: make sure you
buy the uncooked variety for
this dish.

WATCHPOINTS
The macaroni should be
only just tender after
boiling, so it does not become
mushy when heated through in
the oven. It should be completely covered with cheese, so that
the top layer does not become
dry or brittle.

●850 calories per portion

35

Salmon in puff pastry

SERVES 4

1 can (about 7 oz) red salmon (see Buying guide), drained and flaked, skin and bones discarded

$\frac{1}{4}$ cup long-grain rice

salt

2 hard-cooked eggs, chopped

2 tablespoons chopped parsley or snipped chives

$\frac{1}{4}$ cup butter or margarine, melted

2 tablespoons tomato catsup

freshly ground black pepper

1 sheet ($\frac{1}{2}$ a $17\frac{1}{2}$ oz package) frozen puff pastry, thawed

1 small egg, beaten

1 Preheat oven to 425°.

2 Rinse the rice thoroughly under cold running water, then cook in a saucepan of boiling salted water for 12 minutes. Drain and rinse again under cold running water to separate the grains.

3 Put the salmon in a large bowl with the rice, hard-cooked eggs, parsley, melted butter, tomato catsup and salt and pepper to taste. Fold gently to mix, taking care not to break up the pieces of salmon and egg.

4 Roll out the pastry on a floured surface to a rectangle about 14×10 inches. Transfer to a dampened cookie sheet.

5 Place the salmon and rice mixture in the center of the pastry, spreading it out evenly. Dampen the edges of the pastry and press them together over the top of the filling. Crimp the edges and make 3-4 cuts each side.

6 Brush the pastry all over with beaten egg, then bake in the oven for about 40 minutes until golden brown. Carefully transfer to a serving dish and serve hot or cold.

Cook's Notes

 TIME
Preparation about 20 minutes, including cooking the rice and hard-cooking the eggs. Cooking in the oven takes about 40 minutes.

 BUYING GUIDE
Red, rather than pink salmon is recommended for this pastry because of its finer flavor and color.

 WATCHPOINT
If the pastry browns too quickly, cover with foil.

 DID YOU KNOW
This is an easy version of a delicious Russian fish pie, called *kulibyaka*.

●630 calories per portion

Mock paella

SERVES 6

3 kabanos sausages, chopped into
  ½ inch lengths
1 can (about ¾ lb) luncheon meat,
  cut to ½-inch dice
2 tablespoons vegetable oil
1 large onion, chopped
1 large red pepper, seeded and
  chopped
2 cloves garlic, crushed (optional)
6 smoked streaky bacon slices,
  chopped
3 tomatoes, peeled and chopped
1 teaspoon ground turmeric
1½ cups long-grain rice, rinsed
1 cup frozen peas
3 cups chicken broth
2 bay leaves
salt and freshly ground black
  pepper
1 can (about ½ lb) shrimp, drained
lemon wedges, for garnish

1 Heat the oil in a large skillet, add the onion, red pepper and garlic, if using, and sauté gently for 5 minutes until the onion is limp and lightly colored. Add the bacon and continue to cook for 3 minutes, then add the tomatoes and cook for 5 minutes more.

2 Add the chopped kabanos and luncheon meat and continue to cook, stirring, for 2 minutes.

3 Stir in the turmeric, rice and frozen peas. Add about 2½ cups of chicken broth, stir well and add the bay leaves. Season with salt and pepper to taste and simmer gently for 20-25 minutes, stirring occasionally until the rice is tender and the liquid has been absorbed. Stir in the remaining broth, a little at a time, during cooking if the paella begins to look dry and the rice is not quite cooked.

4 Add the shrimp and stir until they are heated through. Discard the bay leaves, transfer the paella to a warmed serving dish and serve at once, garnished with a lemon wedge for each serving.

Cook's Notes

TIME
15 minutes preparation,
35-40 minutes cooking.

SERVING IDEAS
The dish is a meal in itself, but serve with a green salad, if liked.

VARIATIONS
The ingredients can be varied according to taste and what foods you have at hand. For instance, try using left-over chicken or pork instead of the luncheon meat. Add a jar of drained mussels if your budget can stretch to it. A small can of whole kernel corn makes an interesting addition, too.

●705 calories per portion

Pork and mushroom risotto

SERVES 4

¾ lb pork tenderloin, cut into 1-inch cubes
¼ lb bacon slices, cut into ½-inch dice
¼ cup butter or margarine
2 onions, chopped
1 clove garlic, crushed (optional)
1 green pepper, seeded and thinly sliced
1 red pepper, seeded and thinly sliced
1½ cups long-grain rice
about 3 cups hot chicken broth (see recipe)
3 large tomatoes, peeled and chopped
salt and freshly ground black pepper
¼ lb mushrooms, thinly sliced
2 tablespoons chopped fresh parsley
⅓ cup grated Parmesan cheese

1 Sauté the bacon in a large skillet with a lid over moderate heat for 3-4 minutes until the fat runs. Remove the bacon from the pan with a slotted spoon and set aside.

2 Lower heat and melt 3 tablespoons of the butter in the pan. Add the onions and garlic, if using, and sauté gently for 5 minutes until limp and lightly colored. Add the peppers to the pan and sauté, stirring occasionally, for 2 minutes. Remove the vegetables with a slotted spoon and reserve with the bacon.

3 Add the cubes of pork to the pan and sauté, turning often, for 6-8 minutes until evenly and well browned on all sides.

4 Add the rice to the pan and stir to coat all the grains with fat. Stir in the chicken broth. Return the bacon, onions and peppers to the pan, add the tomatoes and season with salt and pepper to taste. Bring to the boil, stir well to mix, then lower the heat, cover and simmer very gently for 40 minutes.

5 Melt the remaining butter in a small saucepan, add the mushrooms and sauté for 1-2 minutes, stirring occasionally.

6 Stir the mushrooms into the risotto. Taste the rice grains – they should be just tender, but not soft. If necessary, cook for a few minutes longer, adding a little more hot broth if needed. Taste and adjust seasoning if necessary.

7 Turn the risotto into a warmed serving dish and sprinkle with the parsley and cheese. Serve at once.

Cook's Notes

TIME
Preparation and cooking take about 1 hour.

WATCHPOINT
To prevent the rice from sticking, it is important that you simmer it very gently. Check from time to time and stir in a little more broth if the dish is drying out: the finished risotto should be moist but not sloppy.

SERVING IDEAS
Perfect accompaniments are salad tossed in oil and lemon juice, and French bread with herb butter.

●670 calories per portion

Lamb pilaf

SERVES 4

1½ cups diced cooked lean lamb
 (see Variations)
1 cup Basmati or long-grain rice
2 tablespoons butter
1¼ cups boiling water
2 tablespoons vegetable oil
1 onion, finely chopped
2 teaspoons curry powder
½ teaspoon turmeric powder
¼ cup currants
¼ cup sliced almonds
2 tomatoes, peeled and chopped
finely grated rind of ½ lemon
1 tablespoon chopped fresh mint
salt and freshly ground black
 pepper
mint leaves, lemon slices and silver
 leaf, for garnish (see Did you
 know)

Cook's Notes

 TIME
Preparation and cooking this dish take about 40 minutes in all.

 DID YOU KNOW
Silver leaf, or *varak*, which is available from Indian food stores, is an edible garnish used in Indian cooking, often in the creamier dishes.

 VARIATIONS
Any cooked meat or poultry may be used and herbs varied accordingly.

●530 calories per portion

1 Rinse the rice thoroughly under cold running water, drain, then place in a large heavy-bottomed saucepan with the butter. Pour in the boiling water, bring back to a boil, then cover with a tight-fitting lid and simmer very gently for about 10 minutes until the water is absorbed and the rice is just tender.

2 Heat the oil in a large skillet, add the onion, curry powder and turmeric and then sauté gently for 5 minutes until the onion is limp. Add the rice and cook the mixture for 5 minutes more, stirring constantly to prevent sticking.

3 Add the lamb, currants and almonds and cook gently for 5 minutes more, stirring constantly. Stir in the tomatoes, lemon rind and mint and cook for 2 minutes more. Season to taste.

4 Pile the lamb pilaf on to a warmed serving dish, garnish with mint leaves, lemon slices and silver leaf. Serve at once.

Mexican beef layer

SERVES 4

½ lb lean ground beef
1 tablespoon vegetable oil
2 onions, finely chopped
4 bacon slices, finely chopped
1 clove garlic, crushed (optional)
1 bay leaf
2 teaspoons tomato paste
1 tablespoon tomato catsup
1 tablespoon golden raisins
1 tablespoon soft brown sugar
½ teaspoon chilli powder
1 cup beef broth
salt
¾ cup Italian risotto rice
1 green pepper, seeded and finely chopped
1 can (about 1 lb) red kidney beans, drained
freshly ground black pepper
margarine, for greasing
1 small avocado pear, for garnish
1¼ cups thick home-made tomato sauce, to serve

1 Heat the oil in a large saucepan, add the chopped onion and the chopped bacon and sauté gently for 5 minutes, until the onion is limp and lightly colored. With a slotted spoon, transfer the onion and bacon to a plate and set aside.

2 Add the ground beef to the pan and sauté over brisk heat for a few minutes until the meat is evenly browned, stirring with a wooden spoon to remove any lumps. Make sure the meat does not stick or burn.

3 Return the onion and bacon to the pan with the garlic, if using, the bay leaf, tomato paste, tomato catsup, raisins, sugar, chili powder and broth. Cover the pan, bring almost to a boil then lower heat and cook very gently for about 30 minutes, stirring occasionally.

4 Meanwhile, bring a large saucepan of salted water to a boil, add the rice and cook for 10 minutes, then add the green pepper and cook for a further 5 minutes or until the rice is tender. Drain.

5 Remove the meat mixture from the heat. Liberally grease a 5-cup pudding mold. Spoon a layer of rice into the mold, followed by a layer of meat mixture, then a layer of beans. Repeat these layers once more, then top with a final layer of rice. Cover the mold with lid or with foil and place in a large saucepan. Pour in boiling water to come halfway up the sides of the mold, cover and simmer the beef layer for 40 minutes.

6 Remove the pudding mold from the saucepan, using pot holders. Cool slightly, remove the foil and run a knife around the mold. Insert a warmed serving plate on top and carefully turn out the beef layer.

7 Peel and slice the avocado pear. Top the beef layer with avocado slices and serve at once, with tomato sauce passed separately.

Cook's Notes

TIME
Preparation takes about 30 minutes. Cooking the beef and rice takes about 30 minutes, layering about 5 minutes and steaming 40 minutes. Turning out the beef layer and topping with the tomato sauce and avocado garnish takes about 5 minutes.

COOK'S TIPS
When turning the steamed dish out, do not worry if it loses shape, it can easily be molded back into place with a knife.

Italian risotto rice gives a creamier result than long-grain and helps the ingredients in the layer to stick together.

●670 calories per portion

Kidney and rice ring

SERVES 6
1½ lb lamb kidneys, cores
    removed, quartered
¼ cup butter
1 large onion, thinly sliced
¼ lb button mushrooms, quartered
4 bacon slices, chopped
2-3 tablespoons all-purpose flour
⅔ cup chicken broth
1-2 tablespoons lemon juice
1 teaspoon tomato paste
½ cup dairy sour cream
salt and freshly ground black
    pepper
paprika, to finish
celery leaves, for garnish

RICE RING
¼ cup butter
1 large onion, chopped
1 teaspoon ground turmeric
1½ cups long-grain rice
3 cups chicken broth
1 bay leaf
butter, for greasing

1 Preheat oven to 350°. Grease a 5-cup ring mold well.
2 Prepare the rice ring: melt half the butter in a flameproof casserole, add the onion and sauté gently for 5 minutes until it is limp and lightly colored. Stir in the turmeric, then add rice. Stir to coat all the grains.
3 Pour the 3 cups chicken broth on to the rice, then add the bay leaf and stir well. Bring to a boil, cover and cook in the oven for 20-30 minutes until the rice is tender and all the broth has been absorbed. Stir in the remaining butter.
4 Pack the cooked rice into the prepared ring mold, pressing it down well. Cover with foil and cook in the oven for 10 minutes.
5 Meanwhile, prepare the kidney filling: melt the butter in a large skillet, add the onion and mushrooms and sauté gently for 5 minutes until the onion is limp and lightly colored. Transfer the onion and the mushrooms to a plate with a slotted spoon.
6 Add the kidneys and bacon to the pan and sauté over moderate heat, stirring frequently, for about 5 minutes until cooked through.

7 Sprinkle in the flour and stir over low heat for 1-2 minutes then gradually stir in the broth, lemon juice to taste and the tomato paste. Simmer, stirring, until the sauce is thick and smooth.
8 Carefully turn the rice mold out on to a warmed serving dish.
9 Stir the onion, mushrooms and sour cream into the kidney mixture. Season to taste. Warm through without boiling and spoon into the center of the rice ring. Sprinkle with paprika, garnish the dish with celery leaves and serve.

Cook's Notes

 TIME
Preparation takes about 15 minutes. Cooking takes about 30 minutes, finishing about 5 minutes.

 SERVING IDEAS
Serve with hot sliced beetroot lightly cooked in creamy horseradish sauce.

●520 calories per portion

41

Ginger chicken

SERVES 4

3 boneless chicken breasts, joints
(each weighing about 7 oz), cut
into 2 × ½-inch strips
2 tablespoons butter or margarine
1 tablespoon vegetable oil
1 large onion, roughly chopped
1 clove garlic, crushed (optional)
3 tablespoons ginger preserve
2 tablespoons soy sauce
1 tablespoon lemon juice
freshly ground black pepper

CORN RICE
¾ cup long-grain rice
salt
1 cup whole kernel corn
¼ cup walnut pieces, roughly
chopped

1 Heat the butter and oil in a skillet
or wok and add the chicken strips,
onion and garlic, if using. Cook
over medium heat, stirring occasionally, for 15 minutes until the
chicken is golden and cooked
through.
2 Meanwhile, cook the rice: bring a
large pan of salted water to a boil,
add the rice, bring back to a boil and
simmer for 5 minutes. Add the corn
and continue cooking for 10 minutes until the rice is tender.
3 Stir the preserve, soy sauce and
lemon juice into the chicken with
pepper to taste. Continue cooking
for 5 minutes more until the ingredients are well blended.
4 Drain the rice mixture and stir in
the chopped walnuts. Transfer to a
warmed serving dish and spoon the
chicken mixture into the center.
Serve at once (see Serving ideas).

Cook's Notes

 TIME
Preparation and cooking
of this dish take about 40
minutes.

WATCHPOINT
Salt should not be neces-
sary in this dish, as the
soy sauce will add enough salt.

 SERVING IDEAS
This quantity of chicken
is enough to make a
light meal with the corn rice
accompaniment. For a more substantial main course dish, use 4
chicken breasts.
Instead of serving with the
rice, serve with pasta shapes.

 VARIATIONS
Chunky orange marma-
lade can be substituted
for the ginger preserve. Use an
11 oz can whole corn instead of
frozen. Heat gently, drain and
stir into rice.

•545 calories per portion

42

Spiced rice chicken

SERVES 4

¾ lb boneless chicken breasts, skinned and cut into 1-inch pieces
¼ cup butter or margarine
1 tablespoon vegetable oil
1 onion, chopped
1 clove garlic, crushed (optional)
1 teaspoon ground cumin
1 teaspoon ground coriander
½ teaspoon ground ginger
½ teaspoon ground turmeric
½ cup orange juice
2 cups chicken broth
¾ cup long-grain rice
⅓ cup seedless raisins
½ cup salted peanuts

1 Preheat oven to 350°.
2 Heat the butter and oil in a skillet, add the chicken pieces and sauté over medium heat until browned on all sides. With a slotted spoon, transfer the chicken to a flameproof serving dish.
3 Add the onion and garlic, if using, to the skillet and sauté gently for 5 minutes until the onion is limp and lightly colored. Stir in the spices, orange juice, chicken broth and the rice. Mix everything together well and bring to the boil.
4 Pour the mixture over the chicken and cook in the oven for about 45 minutes until the chicken and rice are tender. Stir in the raisins and peanuts and serve at once, straight from the dish.

Cook's Notes

TIME
This very quick dish takes 15 minutes to prepare, and about 45 minutes cooking in the oven.

VARIATIONS
Use turkey breasts instead of chicken, and brown rice instead of long-grain. If using brown rice, allow about 15 minutes longer in the oven.

●500 calories per portion

PARTY DISHES

Nasi goreng

Every rice-growing country develops its own special savory rice dishes. This one, *Nasi Goreng*, which means literally fried rice, is a great favorite from Indonesia, where they even eat it for breakfast.

SERVES 4-6
1½ cups long-grain rice
2 cups water
1 tablespoon vegetable oil
1 tablespoon butter
3 shallots, finely sliced
2 red chilis, finely chopped, or ½ teaspoon chili powder
1 clove garlic, crushed (optional)
¼ lb bacon slices or boneless chicken breast, diced
¼ lb button mushrooms, finely sliced
1 teaspoon paprika
1 tablespoon light soy sauce (see Buying guide)
2 teaspoons tomato paste or catsup

FOR GARNISH
cucumber slices
tomato slices
fried onions (see Buying guide) or scallion tops
prawn crackers

1 Rinse the rice thoroughly under cold running water and put it in a large, heavy-based saucepan with a close-fitting lid. Pour in the water (see Cook's tips), bring to a boil, then simmer, uncovered, for 10-15 minutes, until all the water is absorbed. Stir once, then cover the pan tightly and cook for 10 minutes more over the lowest possible heat (see Cook's tips).
2 Spoon the rice on to a large plate, fork it through to separate grains and leave to cool for 2 hours.
3 Heat the oil and butter in a wok or large skillet. Add the shallots, chilis and garlic, if using, and sauté over moderate heat, stirring, for 1-2 minutes. Add the bacon and mushrooms and sauté, stirring, for 2 minutes more. Add the paprika, soy sauce and tomato paste and cook, stirring, for 1 minute, until bacon and mushrooms are tender.
4 Add the rice and stir over gentle heat until heated through. Add salt and a little more soy sauce to taste. Pile the mixture on to a warmed serving dish and garnish with cucumber, tomato, fried onions or scallions and prawn crackers.

Beef cannelloni

SERVES 4-6
16 cannelloni tubes (see Buying
   guide)
¼ cup butter
⅓ cup grated Parmesan cheese
extra butter, for greasing

FILLING
1 lb ground beef
¼ cup butter
1 carrot, finely chopped
½ onion, finely chopped
1 clove garlic, crushed
1 celery stalk, finely chopped
salt and freshly ground black
   pepper
1 tablespoon all-purpose flour
½ cup dry white wine
1 can (about 1 lb) chopped
   tomatoes, drained
½ teaspoon dried oregano
1 tablespoon finely chopped fresh
   parsley

SAUCE
¼ cup butter
½ cup all-purpose flour
2¼ cups milk
freshly grated nutmeg

1 Make the filling: melt the butter
in a saucepan, add the carrot,
onion, garlic, and celery and sauté
gently for 10 minutes until the
onion is browned.
2 Add the ground beef, increase
the heat to medium and sauté until
the meat is evenly browned, stirring
with a wooden spoon to remove
any lumps. Season to taste with salt
and pepper.
3 Lower the heat, then sprinkle in
the flour and stir for 2 minutes.
Remove from the heat and gradually stir in the wine, chopped tomatoes and oregano.
4 Return to the heat, bring to a boil,
then simmer for 20-25 minutes, stirring occasionally, until the meat is
cooked and the sauce has thickened. Remove from the heat, stir in
the parsley, then taste and adjust
seasoning. Leave to cool.
5 Preheat oven to 400°. Grease a
large flameproof dish evenly with
melted butter.
6 Make the sauce: melt the butter in
a saucepan, sprinkle in the flour
and stir over low heat for 1-2 minutes until straw-colored. Remove
from the heat and gradually stir in
the milk. Return to the heat and
simmer, stirring, until thick and
smooth. Season to taste with salt
and pepper to taste and a generous
sprinkling of nutmeg. Remove from
the heat.
7 With a small teaspoon, stuff the
cannelloni with the filling mixture.
Cover the bottom of the dish with a
little of the white sauce, then
arrange the filled cannelloni in a
single row in the dish, separating
each one with a little sauce. Cover
with the remaining sauce, then dot
with the butter and sprinkle with
the Parmesan cheese.
8 Bake in the oven for 20 minutes,
then cover with foil and continue to
cook for 20 minutes more or until
the cannelloni are cooked through.
Serve at once while still piping hot.

Cook's Notes

TIME
50 minutes preparation,
including assembling,
and about 40 minutes cooking in
the oven.

BUYING GUIDE
Buy cannelloni that does
not need pre-cooking.
Instructions are printed on the
package.

FREEZING
Freeze before baking in
the oven. Cool, seal,
label and freeze for up to 3
months. To serve: cook from
frozen in the oven for about 1
hour or until heated right
through.

●690 calories per portion

Chicken timballo

SERVES 4-6

1 lb elbow macaroni
¾ cup uncooked chicken, finely chopped
6 tablespoons butter
½ carrot, finely chopped
½ onion, finely chopped
¼ teaspoon dried thyme
1 celery stalk, finely chopped
¼ lb lean bacon slices cut into thin strips
2 oz button mushrooms, sliced
1 cup dry white wine
salt and freshly ground black pepper
⅓ cup fine bread crumbs, toasted
⅔ cup grated Parmesan cheese

SAUCE
¼ cup butter
½ cup all-purpose flour
1¾ cups milk
freshly grated nutmeg

FOR GARNISH
tomato slices
sprigs of watercress

1 Melt ¼ cup butter in a large saucepan, add the carrot, onion, thyme and celery and sauté gently for 10 minutes.

2 Add the bacon and mushrooms to the pan and continue to sauté for 2 minutes, stirring constantly.

3 Add the chicken to the pan and sauté over medium heat until evenly browned. Stir in the wine and season to taste with salt and pepper. Cover and cook gently for 25 minutes until the chicken is tender.

4 Meanwhile, cook the macaroni: bring a large pan of salted water to a boil. Add the macaroni, bring back to a boil and simmer for about 10 minutes, until tender yet firm.

5 Meanwhile, make the sauce: melt butter in a saucepan, sprinkle in the flour and stir over low heat for 1-2 minutes until straw-colored. Remove from the heat and gradually stir in the milk. Return to the heat and simmer, stirring, until thick and smooth. Season with salt and pepper and a generous sprinkling of nutmeg. Remove from the heat.

6 Drain the macaroni and set aside. Preheat oven to 400°. Grease a 3-quart casserole dish with the remaining butter and coat the bottom and sides with two-thirds of the bread crumbs.

7 Mix the chicken mixture with the macaroni, sauce and Parmesan cheese and turn into the lined dish. Sprinkle the remaining bread crumbs over the top. Cover and cook in the oven for 20 minutes. Turn off the heat and leave in the oven for 5 minutes more. To serve: run a round-bladed knife around the edge of the timballo, then turn out on to a serving plate and garnish with tomato and watercress.

Cook's Notes

TIME
Preparation and cooking take 1¼ hours.

FREEZING
Freeze before baking. Follow instructions for Beef cannelloni.

DID YOU KNOW
A timballo takes its name from the dome-shaped dish in which it is traditionally cooked. It almost always consists of pre-cooked pasta mixed with 1 or 2 sauces and baked in a dish lined with pastry or bread crumbs.

●905 calories per portion

Seafood macaroni bake

SERVES 4

¾ lb fresh or frozen haddock fillets, skinned (see Cook's tips)
2½ cups milk
1 lemon (see Preparation)
1 bay leaf
3 whole black peppercorns
salt
¼ cup butter or margarine
½ lb mushrooms, thinly sliced
2 cups elbow macaroni, boiled, drained and rinsed (see Watchpoint)
1 jar (about 5 oz) mussels, drained
3 tablespoons all-purpose flour
1 package (10 oz) frozen, shelled, deveined shrimp, cooked (see Cook's tips)
pinch of freshly grated nutmeg
freshly ground black pepper
margarine, for greasing
extra lemon slices and shelled fresh shrimp, for garnish (optional)

1 Put the haddock in a large skillet with a lid and pour in enough of the milk to just cover. Add 2 slices of lemon, the bay leaf, peppercorns and a good pinch of salt. Bring gradually to a boil, then cover and turn off the heat under the pan. Leave to stand for 5 minutes, then remove the haddock with a spatula. Flake the flesh into 1½-inch pieces, discarding any bones. Strain all the cooking liquid and reserve it.

2 Melt 1 tablespoon butter in the rinsed-out skillet, add the sliced mushrooms and sauté for 2-3 minutes. Stir in the lemon juice and remove from heat.

3 Preheat oven to 350°.

4 Put the macaroni into a greased large flameproof dish with the haddock, mushrooms and mussels. Stir carefully to mix, without breaking up the fish.

5 Melt the remaining butter in a saucepan, sprinkle in the flour and stir over low heat for 1-2 minutes until straw-colored. Remove from the heat and gradually stir in rest of milk and reserved cooking liquid. Return to the heat and simmer, stirring, until thick and smooth. Remove from heat, stir in the shrimp, nutmeg and salt and pepper to taste, then pour evenly over macaroni and fish mixture in the flameproof dish. Cook in the oven for 20 minutes.

6 Garnish with lemon slices and unpeeled shrimp, if liked, and serve hot, straight from the dish.

48

Peppered pork and shrimp

SERVES 4
½ lb pork tenderloin, trimmed of excess fat, cut into ½-inch cubes
2 tablespoons olive oil
1 red, 1 green and 1 yellow pepper, seeded and cut into 2 × ¼-inch strips (see Buying guide)
1 large onion, chopped
¼ lb frozen, shelled, deveined shrimp, thawed
1 tablespoon dry sherry
1 teaspoon hot pepper sauce
freshly ground black pepper

SPICY NOODLES
6 oz ribbon noodles
salt
1 teaspoon vegetable oil
½ teaspoon ground turmeric
¼ teaspoon ground coriander
¼ teaspoon ground cumin
¼ teaspoon ground ginger

Cook's Notes

 TIME
20 minutes preparation plus about 15 minutes cooking time.

 ECONOMY
Use country-style spare-rib of pork instead of pork tenderloin, but allow ¾ lb as this cut of pork has some bone and more fat. Shoulder of pork steaks can also be used for this recipe.

 VARIATIONS
Thinly sliced good quality steak can be used instead of pork. Or, use cooked meat such as roast pork or chicken and add with the shrimp when the peppers are cooked. Allow another minute or so for heating through.

 BUYING GUIDE
Yellow peppers are difficult to buy, use 2 green peppers and 1 red one.

●375 calories per portion

1 Cook the noodles: bring a large pan of salted water to a boil, swirl in the oil, then add the noodles and the spices. Bring back to a boil and cook for 7-10 minutes until the ribbon noodles are tender yet still firm to the bite.
2 Meanwhile, heat the oil in a skillet, add peppers and onion and cook for 3 minutes, stirring.

3 Add the pork cubes and cook for 8 minutes more, stirring.
4 Stir in the shrimp, sherry and hot pepper sauce, season to taste and cook for 2 minutes.
5 Drain the noodles thoroughly and arrange on 4 warmed serving plates or in individual bowls. Spoon over the pork and shrimp mixture and serve at once.

49

Lamb and pasta medley

SERVES 4
1 lb ground raw lamb
2 tablespoons olive oil
1 onion, chopped
1 green pepper, seeded and
  chopped
2 zucchini, finely chopped
1 can (about 1 lb), chopped
  tomatoes
$1\frac{1}{4}$ cups water
2 cups pasta shapes
$\frac{1}{2}$ teaspoon dried basil
$\frac{1}{2}$ teaspoon dried thyme
salt and freshly ground black
  pepper
$\frac{1}{4}$ lb mushrooms, sliced

1 Heat the oil in a saucepan and sauté the onion, green pepper and zucchini gently for 2-3 minutes until they are beginning to soften. Do not let them begin to brown.

2 Add the lamb, turn the heat to high and sauté until the meat is evenly browned, stirring with a wooden spoon to remove any lumps. Pour off any excess fat and discard it.

3 Stir in the tomatoes with their juice and the water. Bring to the boil, stirring frequently.

4 Add the pasta, herbs and salt and pepper to taste and mix well. Cover the pan and simmer the lamb and pasta for 15 minutes.

5 Stir in mushrooms and simmer, uncovered, for 10 minutes. Serve the lamb and pasta medley at once (see Serving ideas and Variations).

Cook's Notes

 TIME
About 45 minutes to prepare and cook.

 VARIATIONS
Instead of pasta shapes, use any type of pasta you may have. Break up spaghetti into small pieces.

Ground beef can be used as an alternative to the lamb.

Dried mixed herbs may be used instead of the dried basil and thyme.

 SERVING IDEAS
This dish needs no accompaniment, but you can pass grated hard cheese such as Parmesan or Cheddar separately for sprinkling.

 ECONOMY
Use left-over cooked lamb, chopped finely and added with the tomatoes. Omit all of stage 2.

●570 calories per portion

Farmhouse chicken

SERVES 4

4 chicken pieces, each weighing 10-14 oz, skinned
salt and freshly ground black pepper
1 tablespoon butter or margarine
2 tablespoons vegetable oil
¼ lb Italian ribbon noodles
½ lb carrots, cut into 2 × ¼-inch sticks
½ lb frozen sliced green beans, defrosted
2 cans (10 oz) condensed mushroom soup
generous pinch of paprika

1 Preheat oven to 350°.
2 Sprinkle the chicken pieces with salt and pepper. Melt the butter in the oil in a large skillet and cook the chicken over fairly high heat for 5-10 minutes until browned on all sides. Lower the heat and cook for 10-15 minutes more, turning the chicken once during this time.
3 Meanwhile, cook the noodles in boiling salted water for 10-12 minutes until *al dente* (tender yet firm to the bite). Cook the carrots in boiling salted water for 5 minutes until tender.
4 Drain the noodles and carrots thoroughly.
5 In a bowl, mix together the noodles, carrots, green beans and mushroom soup. Spoon this mixture into a large shallow flameproof dish, sprinkle with paprika and place the chicken on top in a single layer.

6 Cover the dish with foil and cook in the oven for 45 minutes or until the chicken is cooked (the juices should run clear when the chicken is pierced with a skewer). Serve hot, straight from the dish.

Cook's Notes

 TIME
This dish takes about 30 minutes to prepare (including pre-cooking the chicken, noodles and carrots). Cooking in the oven takes approximately 45 minutes.

COOK'S TIP
The casserole can be made up to 24 hours in advance, if wished. At the end of stage 5, cover the dish then store in the refrigerator until 1 hour before serving. Cook in the oven as in stage 6 allowing the extra 15 minutes cooking time because it will take that much longer to cook from cold.

 PRESSURE COOKING
Use chicken pieces weighing about ½ lb. Pre-brown chicken in oil, drain. Add 1¼ cups broth and vegetables. Place trivet on top of chicken and put noodles and 1¼ cups water in a perforated separator lined with foil or in a solid separator. Cover with waxed paper and tie down securely. Bring to high (H) pressure and cook for 7 minutes. Release pressure quickly, remove chicken and noodles. Stir in soup, bring to boil and serve on a warmed serving dish.

●495 calories per portion

51

Chicken lasagne

SERVES 4
6 strips lasagne (see Buying guide)
salt
1 teaspoon vegetable oil
freshly ground black pepper
1 cup grated Cheddar cheese
margarine, for greasing

CHICKEN SAUCE
3 tablespoons vegetable oil
1 large onion, sliced
¼ lb bacon slices chopped
¼ cup all-purpose flour
1¼ cups chicken broth
1 can (about ½ lb) chopped
  tomatoes
1½ cups diced cooked chicken (see
  Buying guide)
1 tablespoon tomato paste

WHITE SAUCE
2 tablespoons butter or margarine
¼ cup all-purpose flour
pinch of freshly grated nutmeg
1¼ cups milk

1 Preheat oven to 350° and grease a shallow flameproof dish.
2 Make the chicken sauce: heat the oil in a skillet, add the onion and sauté gently until limp and lightly colored. Add the bacon and cook for 1 minute.
3 Sprinkle in the flour and cook for 1 minute, stirring, until straw-colored. Remove from the heat and gradually stir in broth, tomatoes and their juices, chicken and tomato paste.
4 Return to the heat and bring to a boil, stirring constantly, then lower the heat and simmer for 3 minutes. Remove from the heat and set aside.
5 Bring a large pan of salted water to a boil and cook the lasagne with the oil for 10 minutes.
6 Meanwhile, make the white sauce: melt the butter in a saucepan, sprinkle in the flour and nutmeg and stir over low heat for 2 minutes until straw-colored. Remove from the heat and gradually stir in the milk, return to the heat again and simmer, stirring, until thick and smooth. Set aside.
7 Drain the lasagne and pat dry with absorbent kitchen paper.
8 Spread half the chicken sauce in the bottom of the greased flameproof dish and sprinkle with salt and pepper. Place 3 strips of lasagne on top.
9 Spread the remaining chicken sauce over the lasagne, sprinkle with more salt and pepper and cover with a second layer of lasagne. Pour the white sauce over the lasagne.
10 Sprinkle the grated cheese over the top of the white sauce, then bake in the oven for 1 hour until bubbling and golden. If the topping is not golden at the end of the cooking time, heat the broiler to high and broil the lasagne for 2-3 minutes to brown the cheese.

Cook's Notes

TIME
Preparation 35 minutes, cooking 1 hour.

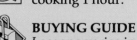
BUYING GUIDE
Lasagne varies in width, from one manufacturer to another – 'strips' of lasagne are narrow; 'sheets' are wider.
  For 1½ cups diced cooked chicken, buy 2 large chicken breasts and cook, skin and bone them before using, or buy half a roasted chicken and simply remove the meat.

FREEZING
Do not pre-cook the lasagne strips. Arrange them over the chicken sauce in layers as in stage 8. Cook the made-up dish in a foil freezer container, cool quickly, then seal, label and freeze. Store for up to 1 month. To serve: reheat from frozen, uncovered, in the foil container in a 400° oven for 1¼ hours until bubbling.

●655 calories per portion

52

Pork and corn stroganoff

SERVES 4

1 lb pork tenderloin, cut into $1\frac{1}{2} \times \frac{1}{4}$-inch strips
freshly ground black pepper
2 tablespoons butter or margarine
2 tablespoons vegetable oil
1 large onion, finely chopped
$\frac{1}{2}$ lb button mushrooms, quartered
1 can whole kernel corn (about 7 oz), drained
$\frac{1}{2}$ cup dairy sour cream
$\frac{1}{4}$ teaspoon freshly grated nutmeg
$\frac{1}{4}$ teaspoon ground cinnamon
salt
paprika, for garnish

1 Season the pork well with pepper.
2 Melt half the butter in half the oil in a shallow flameproof casserole or large heavy-bottomed skillet. Add the onion and sauté gently until browned.

3 Add the mushrooms and toss with the onions for 2-3 minutes until just tender. Transfer the onions and mushrooms with their juices to a dish. Keep warm.
4 Wipe the casserole with kitchen paper, then heat the remaining butter and oil. Add the seasoned pork strips and sauté over brisk heat for 2-3 minutes until sealed on all sides (see Cook's tip). Lower the heat and cook for 15 minutes more, or until

cooked through (when cut in half, the pork strips should not be pink inside).
5 Add the reserved onion and mushroom mixture with the corn and cook over gentle heat for 2 minutes until heated through. Stir in the sour cream, nutmeg, cinnamon and salt to taste. Heat through gently, but do not boil.
6 Transfer to a warmed serving dish and sprinkle with paprika.

Cook's Notes

 TIME
Preparation takes about 15 minutes, cooking about 30 minutes.

 SERVING IDEAS
Serve with noodles, preferably fresh, either plain or wholemeal.

 COOK'S TIP
If necessary, seal the strips of pork in 2 batches to ensure that they are not crowded in the pan: they must be allowed to seal in the shortest possible time. Keep warm while you seal the remainder.

 DID YOU KNOW
This is a variation of the classic Beef Stroganoff – a dish of strips of beef served with dairy sour cream.

●420 calories per portion

Chicken catalan

SERVES 6
6 small chicken breasts, skinned
6 tablespoons olive oil
3 medium onions, thinly sliced
2 cloves garlic, crushed
2 cups long-grain rice
1-2 tablespoons tomato paste
pinch of saffron strands (see Steps)
   or few drops of yellow food
   coloring
2 quarts boiling chicken broth
1 teaspoon paprika
salt and ground black pepper
¼ lb Spanish chorizo sausage or
   other firm garlic sausage
   (optional), cut into large pieces
1 green pepper, seeded and sliced
   into rings
1 red pepper, seeded and sliced
   into rings
1 cup stuffed green olives
chopped parsley, for garnish

1 Heat half the oil in large flame-proof casserole. Cook the chicken breasts over medium heat until golden brown in color and half cooked through (about 7 minutes each side).
2 Remove chicken pieces and keep them warm.
3 Add 1 tablespoon more oil to the casserole. Sauté the onions over low heat for 2 minutes until transparent but not brown.
4 Add the garlic, the remaining oil and the rice. Stir for a few minutes with wooden spoon until the rice starts to color.
5 Meanwhile, stir the tomato paste and coloring, if used, into the boiling broth.
6 Stir broth, with saffron liquid, if used, into the rice mixture, add paprika and salt and pepper to taste, then bring to a boil, stirring constantly.
7 Add the chicken to the casserole with the sausage and peppers, pressing all these well down into the rice.

8 Lower the heat, cover and simmer for about 30 minutes or until the rice is just tender, stirring occasionally with a wooden spoon. Be careful not to overcook the rice or it will become mushy.
9 Add the olives to the rice and heat through for a few minutes. Taste and adjust seasoning.
10 Transfer to a large warmed serving dish. Sprinkle the chopped parsley over the top to garnish and serve at once.

Cook's Notes

 TIME
10-15 minutes for preparation plus 1 hour cooking.

 ECONOMY
Chicken breasts are meaty and convenient to use, because they are sold boneless or partially boned, but they do tend to be rather expensive. Ordinary chicken pieces are not so expensive as breasts, and they can be used just as well but will need to be cooked for about 10 minutes on each side in stage 1. (You could even buy a whole broiler/fryer and joint it yourself.) If you prefer not to have awkward-looking bones in the finished dish, it is very simple to remove the bones before the chicken is cooked.

DID YOU KNOW
Saffron is an immensely popular spice in Spain, where it is used for coloring rice (it has hardly any taste). It was introduced to the Spaniards by the Arabs, and has for centuries been used as a coloring agent, especially in Arab and Eastern cooking. It is used in this recipe to give the rice a bright golden-yellow color, but as it is so expensive, we have suggested yellow food coloring as a cheaper alternative. If you have ground turmeric this can also be used, but it has a more distinctive flavor than saffron. Saffron strands and turmeric are available from delicatessens, good supermarkets and Indian specialist stores.

BUYING GUIDE
Spanish chorizo sausages can be obtained at most good delicatessens, and are easily recognizable by their bright red appearance. They are made from pure pork flavored with pimiento (hot red pepper), and so are hot and spicy. If you find them difficult to obtain, use any cured sausage with a spicy flavor.

●330 calories per portion

54

HOW TO USE SAFFRON

 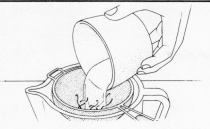 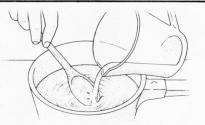

1 *Crush a few strands of saffron in your fingers and drop them into a small bowl of boiling water.*

2 *Leave to infuse for at least 2 hours, then strain the water, discarding the saffron strands.*

3 *Stir the saffron-colored liquid into the broth used in recipe.*

Spanish beef casserole

SERVES 4

1 lb stewing beef, cut into 1½-inch cubes
2 tablespoons olive or vegetable oil
1 onion, chopped
1 clove garlic, crushed (optional)
1 can (about 1 lb) chopped tomatoes
1 red pepper, seeded and chopped
2 tablespoons medium sherry
8 stuffed green olives, halved
1 thyme sprig or ½ teaspoon dried thyme
salt and freshly ground black pepper

TOPPING

1 tablespoon butter
1 small onion, finely chopped
¾ cup long-grain rice
1¼ cups boiling water
1 tablespoon grated Parmesan cheese

1 Preheat oven to 350°.

2 Heat olive oil in large flameproof casserole, add the onion, garlic, if using, and the stewing steak and sauté for 5 minutes.

3 Add the tomatoes, half the red pepper, the sherry, green olives and thyme, and season well with salt and pepper. Bring to a boil, cover, then transfer to the oven and cook for 1¼ hours.

4 Meanwhile, make the topping: melt the butter in a large saucepan, add the onion and sauté gently for about 5 minutes until limp.

5 Add the rice and stir until coated with butter. Add the remaining red pepper and season with salt. Add the boiling water, then cover and simmer for about 10-15 minutes, until the rice is tender and all the liquid has evaporated. Remove from heat and stir in cheese.

6 Spread the topping evenly over the meat in the casserole. Return to the oven and cook, uncovered, for 20 minutes more. Serve at once, straight from the casserole.

Summer pork curry

SERVES 4

1¼ lb shoulder butt pork, trimmed of fat, cut into 1-inch cubes (see Buying guide)
¼ cup butter or margarine
2 large onions, sliced
2 cloves garlic, crushed (optional)
1 teaspoon ground ginger
1 teaspoon ground turmeric
1 teaspoon chili powder
2 teaspoons ground cumin
2 teaspoons paprika
1 tablespoon ground coriander
2 tablespoons cornstarch
1¼ cups chicken broth
salt and ground black pepper
2 small bananas, thinly sliced
1 large peach, thinly sliced
coriander sprigs, to garnish

CARDAMOM RICE

1 cup Basmati rice or other long-grain rice
¼ cup butter
3 cardamom pods, crushed
2 bay leaves
2½ cups water

1 Melt the butter in a large flameproof casserole, add onions and the garlic, if using, and sauté gently for 5 minutes until limp and lightly colored. Add the pork and cook over medium heat, stirring often, until lightly browned on all sides. Stir in the spices and cook for 1-2 minutes more.

2 In a small bowl, blend the cornstarch with a little broth to make a smooth paste. Stir in the remaining broth, then add to the casserole and bring to a boil, stirring constantly, until thick and smooth.

3 Cover and simmer gently for 1¼-1½ hours until pork is tender when pierced with a sharp knife.

4 About 20 minutes before the end of cooking time, make cardamom rice: wash the rice and drain it well. Melt the butter in a large saucepan. Add the rice with the cardamoms and bay leaves and cook gently for 3-4 minutes, stirring well. Pour the water into the pan and bring to a boil. Cover and simmer gently for 10-15 minutes or until rice is tender and the water is absorbed. Discard the cardamoms and bay leaves. Season the rice to taste with pepper and spoon it evenly into a warmed serving bowl.

5 Remove the curry from the heat and gently stir in the banana slices, taking care not to break them up. Arrange the peach slices along one side of the casserole. Garnish with coriander sprigs and serve at once, accompanied by the cardamom rice.

Cook's Notes

TIME
Preparing the curry takes 25-30 minutes, cooking 1¼-1½ hours.

SERVING IDEAS
Serve with spicy or plain poppadoms, which are available in packages from Indian stores. Pass a bowl of peach or mango chutney separately with the curry.

BUYING GUIDE
Shoulder butt, one of the less expensive pork cuts, comes from the upper part of the shoulder. It is excellent for casseroled dishes and also for making kabobs.

●910 calories per portion

Paella

The basic essential ingredients for every paella are long-grain rice, olive oil and saffron. After that it can be simple or elaborate according to the ingredients you use. Vary these to suit your budget as well as your taste.

You can serve it for a simple summer lunch, or dress it up as a more elaborate, but easy-to-prepare party dish. Paella is perfect for a buffet, as it can so easily be eaten with a fork.

SERVES 6

12 unshucked mussels, thawed if frozen (see Steps), or 1 can or jar (about 5 oz), drained
2 lb boiler/fryer, cut into 8 pieces
¼ lb pork tenderloin cut into ½-inch cubes
salt and freshly ground black pepper
½ cup olive oil
2 raw chorizo sausages, cut into ¼-inch slices
1 onion, finely chopped
2 cloves garlic, crushed (optional)
1 red pepper, seeded and cut into 1½ × ¼-inch strips
½ lb tomatoes, peeled, seeded and finely chopped
1 teaspoon paprika
2 cups long-grain rice
½ teaspoon saffron strands, crushed and soaked for 2 hours in 1 quart boiling hot chicken broth
½ lb unshelled, cooked shrimp, thawed if frozen (see Buying guide), or ¼ lb shelled shrimp, thawed if frozen, or 1 can (about 7 oz) shelled shrimp, drained
1 can (14 oz) artichoke hearts, drained
½ lb frozen peas, thawed

1 If using unshucked mussels, prepare them as shown in the Steps.
2 Cook the prepared mussels: rinse the soaked mussels thoroughly, then drain. Pour ½ cup water into a heavy skillet large enough to hold the mussels in a single layer. Add the mussels, cover and bring to a boil then lower the heat and simmer for 5-6 minutes, shaking the pan gently once or twice. If the mussels have not opened, cook for 1-2 minutes longer. Discard any unopened mussels and set the rest on one side.
3 Season the chicken pieces and pork cubes with salt and pepper. Heat half the oil in a paella pan (see Did you know), large skillet, or large, shallow flameproof casserole. Add the chicken and pork and cook over medium heat for 10-15 minutes, turning frequently, until browned on all sides. After 5 minutes cooking, add the sausage slices to the pan and turn to brown. With a slotted spoon, lift out the meats on to a plate and set aside.
4 Heat the remaining oil in the pan. Add the onion, garlic, if using, pepper strips and chopped tomatoes and cook over gentle heat for about 5 minutes, stirring from time to time, until the onion is limp and the mixture well blended. Stir in the paprika. Cook for 1 minute. Remove from heat. Stir in rice.
5 Strain the saffron broth into the pan and stir once. Bring to the boil and cook for 5 minutes.
6 Arrange the chicken, pork, sausages, cooked mussels, shrimp and artichoke hearts on top of the rice. Sprinkle over the peas.
7 Turn down heat to low. Cook for 12-15 minutes, until rice is tender and all liquid absorbed.
8 Turn off the heat under the pan. Cover the pan with a lid or drape it with a dish-towel. Leave for 3-4 minutes, to allow the flavors to blend. Serve straight from the pan.

TO CLEAN MUSSELS

1 *Check mussels are fresh: tap open ones against work surface. Discard if they do not shut.*

2 *Pull away any beards (pieces of hanging seaweed gripped between the 2 shells of the mussel).*

3 *Scrub under cold running water, then scrape away incrustations. Soak mussels in fresh cold water for 2-3 hours. Change the water several times.*

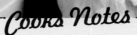
Cooks Notes

TIME
Preparation takes about 1¼ hours if using un-shucked mussels. Allow 2-3 hours more for soaking the mussels and saffron threads. Cooking the paella takes about 45 minutes.

WATCHPOINT
It is absolutely vital to discard any unopened mussels – this shows they are not fresh, which can cause serious food poisoning.

BUYING GUIDE
Try to buy mussels and shrimp in the shell, as they look so attractive in the finished dish. Both are available from high-quality fish suppliers, and frozen from freezer centers and some supermarkets.

SERVING IDEAS
Serve the paella at the table straight from the pan, as the Spaniards do.

The paella is usually eaten by itself – a vegetable accompaniment is not necessary.

VARIATIONS
In Spain, paella is often made with rabbit, and this could be substituted for the chicken in this recipe.

For a special occasion, add some lobster meat to the paella.

DID YOU KNOW
The name paella comes from *paellera*, the pan in which the dish is traditionally cooked in Spain: it is shallow with gently sloping sides and 2 flattened handles. You can buy special paella pans from high-quality kitchen equipment stores or departments of big stores – or, better still, buy one on holiday in Spain. But if you do not have a *paellera*, a large heavy skillet, preferably with a lid, or a large, shallow flameproof casserole will do very well instead for making the paella.

● 980 calories per portion

Spicy roast chicken

SERVES 4-6
3-3½ lb boiler/fryer
2 tablespoons butter, softened
1 teaspoon ground turmeric
1 teaspoon ground ginger
¼ teaspoon cayenne
vegetable oil, for greasing

STUFFING
2 tablespoons vegetable oil
1 onion, finely chopped
1 large red pepper, seeded and
  finely chopped
2 garlic cloves, crushed (optional)
½ cup long-grain rice
1½ cups hot chicken broth
¼ cup sliced almonds
finely grated rind of 1 lime
1 tablespoon fresh lime juice
½ teaspoon ground turmeric
½ teaspoon ground ginger
¼ teaspoon cayenne
salt and freshly ground black
  pepper

1 Make the stuffing: heat the oil in a saucepan, add the onion, red pepper and garlic, if using, and sauté gently for 5 minutes until the onion is limp and lightly colored. Add the rice and cook for 1-2 minutes, stirring constantly, then pour in the hot broth. Bring to a boil, stir once, then lower the heat, cover and simmer very gently for about 20 minutes until the rice is cooked and all the liquid has been absorbed.

2 Transfer the rice and vegetables to a bowl, stir in the remaining stuffing ingredients with salt and pepper to taste and leave to cool.

3 Preheat oven to 375° and grease a small flameproof dish.

4 Wipe the chicken inside and out with kitchen paper. Spoon about one-third of the stuffing mixture into the neck end of the chicken. Fold the neck skin back into position, then fold the wing tips over it. Secure with a metal skewer. Spoon the remaining stuffing into the prepared dish. Cover with foil.

5 Place the chicken in a roasting pan. Prick the skin all over, except for the stuffed area. Mix the butter and spices, with salt and pepper to taste, and brush over chicken.

6 Roast the prepared chicken in the oven for about 1½ hours, until tender (the juices run clear when the thigh is pierced with a skewer). Baste the chicken occasionally. Halfway through cooking time, place the dish of stuffing on the shelf below the chicken to cook.

7 Transfer the chicken to a warmed serving dish, remove the skewer and keep the chicken warm in the oven turned to its lowest setting. Skim the fat from the juices in the roasting pan and pour juices over chicken. Serve carved into slices, with stuffing (see Serving ideas).

Cook's Notes

 TIME
Preparing the stuffing takes about 25 minutes. Allow 30 minutes for cooling. Preparation then takes 10 minutes, cooking 1½ hours.

 COOK'S TIP
The stuffing can be made ahead of time, but to avoid any risk of food poisoning it should not be used to stuff the chicken until just before roasting. There should always be a free circulation of air in the center of the bird.

 SERVING IDEAS
Serve with a stir-fried mixture of vegetables such as cauliflower flowerets, bean sprouts and carrot strips.

●645 calories per portion

60

Lamb chops in tomato rice

SERVES 4

4 lamb loin or shoulder chops,
   trimmed of excess fat
1 tablespoon butter or margarine
2 tablespoons vegetable oil
1 onion, chopped
1 celery stalk, chopped
1 can (about 1 lb) chopped tomatoes
1¼ cups water
1 cup long-grain rice
1 tablespoon chopped fresh basil or
   1 teaspoon dried basil
salt and freshly ground black
   pepper
basil sprigs, to garnish (optional)

1 Melt the butter in the oil in a large skillet with a lid. Add the chops and sauté over brisk heat for 5-10 minutes, turning once, to brown on both sides. Remove from the pan and set aside.

2 Add the onion and celery to the pan and sauté gently for 5 minutes until limp and lightly colored. Stir in the tomatoes with their juice, add the water and bring to a boil.

3 Add the rice, basil and seasoning and stir well. Return the chops to the pan and cover with the tomato and rice mixture.

4 Cover the pan and simmer gently for 30-40 minutes or until the chops are cooked through (the juices should run clear when chops are pierced with a sharp knife), the rice is tender and all the liquid has been absorbed. Fluff up the rice.

5 Taste and adjust seasoning. Transfer to a warm serving dish and garnish with basil sprigs, if liked. Serve at once.

Cook's Notes

 TIME
Preparation takes about 10 minutes, cooking 45-55 minutes.

 COOK'S TIP
This dish needs no vegetable accompaniment, but serve a green salad and vinaigrette to follow.

 VARIATIONS
The flavor of basil goes especially well with tomatoes, but if unavailable, thyme would also be good.

Pork chops may be used instead of lamb, in which case substitute sage for the basil.

●780 calories per portion

Apricot-stuffed lamb

SERVES 8
4 lb boneless shoulder of lamb, with bones reserved (see Buying guide)
1 teaspoon ground coriander

STUFFING
2 tablespoons vegetable oil
1 onion, finely chopped
¼ cup long-grain rice, cooked
¼ lb dried apricots, soaked overnight, drained and chopped
finely grated rind of 1 large orange
1 tablespoon ground coriander
salt and freshly ground black pepper

FOR GARNISH
apricot halves
mint sprigs

1 Preheat oven to 400°.
2 Make the stuffing: heat the oil in a saucepan, add the onion and sauté gently for 5 minutes until limp and lightly colored. Remove from the heat, add the rice, apricots, orange rind, coriander and salt and pepper to taste and stir all the ingredients to mix very thoroughly.

3 Open out the lamb and lay it skin side down on a board or work surface. Sprinkle with the coriander and season with salt and pepper, then spoon the stuffing into the boned cavity, packing it in well. Fold the 2 long sides of the lamb over the stuffing to overlap and form into a neat roll (see Preparation). Tie the stuffed rolled lamb at intervals with fine string.

4 Place the lamb bones in a roasting pan. Set a meat rack over the bones and place the lamb on the rack. Roast in the oven for 30 minutes, then lower the heat to 350° and roast for 1½ hours more until the lamb is tender and cooked through (the juices run clear when the meat is pierced with a fine skewer; if pink, give a little more cooking).

5 Remove the string and transfer the lamb to a warmed serving dish. Leave in a warm place for 10 minutes to allow the meat to 'settle', to make it easier to carve.

6 Carve the lamb into slices, garnish with apricot halves and mint sprigs. Serve the lamb at once, with a gravy made from the pan juices passed separately in a warmed sauceboat.

Cook's Notes

 TIME
Preparation takes about 35 minutes. Cooking takes 2 hours. Allow about 5 minutes for making the gravy and finishing the dish.

 BUYING GUIDE
It is best to order the meat in advance so the butcher will have time to prepare it. The bones, placed under the meat as it is cooking, help enrich the gravy.

 PREPARATION
To roll the boned lamb after stuffing:

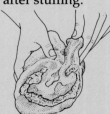

Fold 2 long sides of meat over the stuffing to overlap, then form it into a neat roll.

●500 calories per portion

62

Moroccan stuffed lamb

SERVES 4-6

4 lb boneless shoulder of lamb, trimmed and tied
2 tablespoons butter or margarine
1 small onion, chopped
1 clove garlic, crushed (optional)
1 celery stalk, chopped
¾ cup water
¼ cup long-grain rice
¼ teaspoon ground cardamom
2 tablespoons chopped fresh mint or 1 tablespoon dried mint
salt and freshly ground black pepper
3 tablespoons sliced almonds, toasted
2-3 tablespoons seedless raisins
1 egg, beaten

1 Preheat oven to 450°.
2 Melt the butter in a small skillet. Add the onion, garlic, if using, and celery and sauté for 5 minutes over gentle heat until limp and lightly colored. With a slotted spoon, transfer to a bowl.
3 Bring the water to a boil in a saucepan. Add the rice, cardamom, half the mint and salt to taste and stir well. Cover the pan and simmer very gently for 15-20 minutes or until the rice is tender and all the water has been absorbed.
4 Mix the rice with the vegetables in the bowl and stir in the almonds, raisins and the remaining mint. Season to taste. Mix in the egg to bind, forking it through the ingredients.
5 Spoon the stuffing into the cavity in the lamb. Roll up snugly and tie at intervals with fine string.
6 Place the lamb, fat side up, on a meat rack in a roasting pan. Roast in the oven for 20 minutes, then lower the heat to 350°. Continue roasting for 1-1½ hours or until the lamb is cooked to your liking (for medium-done meat the juices run slightly pink when the meat is pierced).

7 Remove the string and leave the lamb to 'rest' for 10 minutes before carving (this makes carving easier). Transfer the lamb to a warmed serving platter to carve.

SNACKS AND SAUCES

Tortellini with tomato sauce

SERVES 4
1 lb tortellini (see Buying guide)
salt
4 slices processed cheese (see For children)

SAUCE
1 can (about 1 lb) tomatoes
1 onion, chopped
few sprigs parsley
2 tablespoons margarine
¼ cup all-purpose flour
1 teaspoon tomato paste
1 teaspoon honey
salt and ground black pepper

1 Make sauce. Blend the tomatoes and their juices, onion and the parsley sprigs to a purée.
2 Melt the margarine in a saucepan, sprinkle in the flour and stir over low heat for 1-2 minutes. Gradually stir in the puréed mixture, then add tomato paste and honey. Season to taste with salt and pepper. Simmer very gently for 20 minutes, stirring occasionally, until the sauce is thick and quite smooth.
3 Meanwhile, bring a large pan of salted water to a boil and cook the tortellini for 3-4 minutes if fresh (or according to package instructions, if dried). Heat the broiler to high. Drain pasta thoroughly and divide between 4 individual flame proof dishes. Pour over the tomato sauce and put a cheese slice on top. Put the dishes under the broiler for about 3 minutes until cheese has melted. Serve at once.

Cook's Notes

TIME
Preparing and cooking take only 45 minutes.

BUYING GUIDE
Tortellini makes a very useful standby for a quick snack or supper dish. Fresh tortellini are sold loose or packed in plastic boxes from delicatessens and some large supermarkets. They can be either plain or green and stuffed with either a meat or cheese filling. Dried varieties are sold in packages at most supermarkets. All are suitable for this dish.

FOR CHILDREN
Use animal-shaped or other fancy cookie cutters to cut cheese slices into fun shapes. But watch the broiling – if the cheese melts too much the figures will lose their shapes.

●380 calories per portion

Crispy stuffed cannelloni

SERVES 4
8 cannelloni tubes (see Buying guide)
salt
1½ tablespoons vegetable oil
1 onion, finely chopped
¾ cup cream cheese
½ cup finely chopped ham
½ cup finely chopped walnuts
2 teaspoons tomato paste
8 ripe olives, pitted and chopped
2 tablespoons chopped fresh parsley
freshly ground black pepper
1 egg
3 tablespoons fresh bread crumbs
2 tablespoons grated Parmesan cheese
vegetable oil, for deep-frying

1 Bring a large pan of salted water to a boil. Add 1 tablespoon of the oil and then the cannelloni. Bring back to a boil, lower the heat and simmer for 4-5 minutes. Drain, rinse under cold water, pat dry and let cool.

2 Heat the remaining oil in a skillet, add the onion and sauté gently for 10 minutes until soft and browned. Remove from the pan with a slotted spoon and drain on kitchen paper for a few minutes.

3 Beat the cream cheese in a bowl until smooth. Beat in the fried onion, chopped ham, walnuts, tomato paste, olives and parsley. Season to taste with salt and pepper and mix well.

4 Using a teaspoon, push spoonfuls of the mixture into the cannelloni tubes, filling them evenly (see Preparation).

5 Beat the egg in a shallow dish. Mix the bread crumbs and Parmesan cheese together on a large flat plate. Dip the cannelloni tubes into the egg; then roll them in the bread crumbs and cheese until evenly coated with the mixture.

6 Pour enough oil into a deep-fat fryer to cover the cannelloni tubes. Heat to 375° or until a stale bread cube browns in 50 seconds.

7 Using a slotted spoon, lower 4 cannelloni at a time into the hot oil and deep-fry for 2-3 minutes until golden brown on all sides. Drain on kitchen paper and keep warm while frying remainder. Serve hot.

Cook's Notes

TIME
The stuffed tubes take about 20 minutes to pre-cook and prepare. Frying time is 4-6 minutes.

PREPARATION
To fill the cannelloni tubes for frying:

Use a teaspoon to fill the cannelloni tubes – gently push in the mixture.

BUYING GUIDE
Be sure to buy the cannelloni that are for boiling not those for baked dishes.

SERVING IDEAS
Serve with a green salad or, to make a more substantial supper dish, with French fries as well.

VARIATIONS
Use cottage or ricotta cheese instead of cream cheese if you prefer.

●430 calories per portion

Pasta kugel

SERVES 4
2 cups wholemeal pasta rings
3 eggs
1 cup cream cheese
½ cup dairy sour cream
2 tablespoons soft brown sugar
⅔ cup seedless raisins
¼ teaspoon salt
¼ teaspoon ground cinnamon
¼ teaspoon freshly grated nutmeg
margarine, for greasing

TOPPING
2 tablespoons chopped mixed nuts
¼ teaspoon ground cinnamon
1 tablespoon butter

1 Preheat oven to 350°. Grease a 5-cup flameproof dish generously with margarine.
2 Bring a pan of salted water to the boil and cook the pasta rings for 12 minutes or according to package instructions until they are cooked but still firm to the bite.
3 Meanwhile, beat the eggs in a bowl, add the cream cheese, soured cream and sugar and beat with a fork until smooth. Mix in the raisins, salt and spices.
4 Drain the cooked pasta rings and return them to the rinsed-out pan. Pour the cream cheese mixture over the pasta and stir it until evenly coated. Transfer the mixture to the prepared dish, sprinkle with nuts and cinnamon and dot the surface with the butter.
5 Bake in the oven, uncovered, for about 30 minutes, until the top is golden and filling has set around the edge but is still creamy in the middle. Serve at once straight from the dish (see Serving ideas).

Cook's Notes

 TIME
20 minutes preparation and about 30 minutes baking in the oven.

 DID YOU KNOW
Kugel is the Jewish name for a pudding, usually made of noodles or potatoes and baked. Although many kugels, like this one, are semi-sweet, they are not meant to be served as desserts.

 SERVING IDEAS
This wholemeal pasta kugel makes a tasty brunch, lunch or supper dish, served with green salad or fruit, such as sliced pears or peaches.

 VARIATION
Other pasta shapes can be used instead of rings, such as shells or wheels.

●535 calories per portion

66

Spaghetti with meat balls

SERVES 4
¾ lb spaghetti
3 tablespoons vegetable oil
1 onion, chopped
1 clove garlic, crushed (optional)
1 can (about 14 oz) tomatoes
⅓ cup hot chicken broth
1 tablespoon tomato paste
¼ teaspoon dried thyme
1 teaspoon dried oregano
salt and freshly ground black
  pepper
1 lb ground beef
2 tablespoons chopped fresh
  parsley
a knob of butter, for tossing
grated Parmesan cheese (optional)

1 Heat 1 tablespoon oil in a large saucepan, add the onion and garlic, if using, and sauté gently for 5 minutes until limp and lightly colored. Add the tomatoes with their liquid, the broth, tomato paste, thyme and half the oregano. Season to taste. Bring to a boil, cover and simmer for 30-40 minutes.

2 Meanwhile, in a bowl mix the beef with the remaining oregano and the parsley and season well. Shape into 32 small balls.

3 Heat the rest of the oil in a skillet over medium heat and sauté the meat balls on all sides for 6-8 minutes until golden brown. Drain on kitchen paper and keep warm.

4 Bring a pan of salted water to a boil and cook the spaghetti for about 10 minutes until *al dente* (tender, yet firm to the bite).

5 Meanwhile, sieve the tomato sauce, or purée in a blender. Return to the pan to reheat, adding a little water if the sauce is too thick. Stir in the meat balls and then transfer to a warmed serving dish.

6 Drain the pasta thoroughly and toss in butter. Transfer to warmed individual serving bowls. Spoon 8 meat balls and a quarter of the sauce over each spaghetti serving. Serve at once, with cheese, if liked.

Cook's Notes

TIME
This dish takes about 1 hour in all to prepare and cook.

SERVING IDEAS
This dish makes a very filling lunch on its own. For dinner, serve with some crusty white bread and a crisp green salad.

VARIATION
Instead of the broth use the same quantity of red wine and perhaps drink the rest with the meal!

●685 calories per portion

Spaghetti alla bolognese

SERVES 4
1 lb spaghetti
2 tablespoons vegetable oil
1 bacon slice, finely chopped
1 small onion, finely chopped
2-inch piece of carrot, finely chopped
2-inch piece of celery, finely chopped
1 clove garlic, finely chopped (optional)
¾ lb finely ground lean beef (see Buying guide)
4 tablespoons dry red wine or beef broth
½ lb plum tomatoes, chopped, or 1 can (½ lb) chopped tomatoes with their juice
pinch of freshly grated nutmeg
¼ – ½ teaspoon dried oregano
salt and freshly ground black pepper
⅓ cup grated Parmesan cheese, to serve

1 Heat the oil in a large skillet, add the bacon, onion, carrot, celery and garlic, if using, and sauté over medium heat for about 10 minutes until the vegetables are softened, stirring occasionally.
2 Add the beef, raise the heat and cook until the meat is evenly browned on all sides, stirring with a wooden spoon to remove any lumps.
3 Stir in the wine and bring to a boil, then lower the heat again and simmer for about 10-15 minutes until the wine has reduced.
4 Stir in the tomatoes with their juice and bring to a boil. Lower the heat, add the nutmeg, oregano and salt and pepper to taste, and cook for about 30 minutes, stirring occasionally. Add more water if the sauce becomes too dry.
5 Meanwhile, cook the spaghetti in a large saucepan of boiling salted water for 10-12 minutes or until *al dente* (tender, yet firm to the bite).
6 Drain thoroughly, transfer to a warmed serving dish and pour the sauce over. Serve sprinkled with grated Parmesan cheese.

Cook's Notes

TIME
About 10 minutes to prepare and about 1 hour to cook.

FREEZING
The bolognese sauce freezes extremely well: transfer to a rigid container, leaving headspace, cool quickly then seal, label and freeze for up to 3 months. To serve: put frozen sauce in a heavy-bottomed saucepan with 1-2 tablespoons water and heat gently until bubbling, stirring frequently.

BUYING GUIDE
The secret of making a good bolognese sauce which is smooth in texture, lies in the quality of the beef. Buy a piece of chuck and grind it at home for the best results.

•705 calories per portion

Frankfurter and macaroni supper

SERVES 4
**6 frankfurters, cut into 1-inch
  lengths**
salt
1½ cups elbow macaroni
2 tablespoons vegetable oil
2 onions, sliced
**1 green pepper, seeded and
  chopped**
**2 tomatoes, peeled, seeded and
  chopped**
1 tablespoon cornstarch
½ cup plain yogurt
1 tablespoon tomato paste
¼ teaspoon dried mixed herbs
freshly ground black pepper
2-3 tablespoons milk (optional)

FOR GARNISH
**2 tomatoes, peeled and sliced
parsley sprigs**

1 Preheat oven to 425°.
2 Bring a pan of salted water to the
boil, add the macaroni and cook for
about 15 minutes until just tender.
3 Meanwhile, heat the oil in a large
skillet, add the onions, green pepper and frankfurters and sauté over
medium heat for 5 minutes, or until
the onions are limp and lightly
colored. Stir in the tomatoes and
cook, stirring occasionally, for 5
minutes more.
4 Put the cornstarch into a bowl
and blend to a smooth paste with
1-2 tablespoons of yogurt. Gradually stir in the remaining yogurt,
then the tomato paste, herbs and
salt and pepper to taste.
5 Pour the mixture over the vegetables in the skillet and bring to a
boil, stirring constantly. Remove
from the heat.
6 Drain the macaroni, rinse under
hot running water, then drain again
thoroughly and add to the vegetable mixture, folding it in carefully.
Add a little milk if the sauce seems
too thick.
7 Transfer the mixture to a 6-cup
flameproof casserole and bake in
the oven, uncovered, for 10-15
minutes (see Cook's tip).
8 Garnish with the tomato slices
and a few parsley sprigs, then serve
hot, straight from the casserole.

Cook's Notes

TIME
This dish takes a total of
45 minutes to prepare
and cook.

FREEZING
At the end of stage 6,
transfer to a rigid con-
tainer, cool quickly, cover then
seal, label and freeze for up to 3
months. To serve: thaw at room
temperature for 4 hours, then
turn into a casserole and continue from the beginning of
stage 7, allowing an extra 10
minutes or so baking time.

COOK'S TIP
The dish can be finished
off under a pre-heated
medium broiler, rather than in
the oven, as long as the mixture
is kept hot during each stage of
preparation.

DID YOU KNOW
This dish is often called
Frank and Mac from the
shortened names of the two
main ingredients.

●435 calories per portion

Deep-fried ravioli

MAKES 30
2 cups all-purpose flour
large pinch salt
¼ cup butter, diced
2 eggs, separated
⅓ cup water
vegetable oil, for deep frying
basil leaves, for garnish

FILLING
¾ cup grated Swiss cheese
½ cup finely chopped cooked ham
1 tablespoon finely chopped fresh parsley
1 tablespoon chopped fresh basil
1 egg
salt and ground black pepper

1 Make the filling: mix together the cheese, ham and herbs in a medium-sized bowl. In another bowl beat the egg with a little salt and freshly ground black pepper. Cover both and refrigerate until needed.

2 Sift the flour and salt into a large bowl. Add the butter and cut it in with two knives until the mixture resembles fine bread crumbs. Make a well in the center, add egg yolks and water and mix to a soft dough that is easy to handle.

3 Turn out on to a lightly floured surface and knead gently until dough is no longer sticky. Roll out to a rectangle about 15 × 10 inches and cut out about thirty 2½ inch circles using a cookie cutter.

4 Lightly beat the egg whites. Brush the edges of the circles with the egg whites and place a teaspoon of the filling in the center of each one. Fold over the edges to form semicircles. Press the edges together to seal firmly for frying.

5 Meanwhile, pour enough oil into a deep-fat fryer with a basket to come halfway up the sides. Heat the oil to 375° or until a stale bread cube turns golden in 50 seconds. Fry ravioli in batches of 10, until golden brown.

6 Remove each batch and drain on kitchen paper. Fry the remaining ravioli, reheating the oil between batches. Pile the cooked ravioli on to a serving plate and serve at once, garnish with basil leaves.

Cook's Notes

TIME
Making the dough and filling takes 15 minutes. Filling the ravioli with its cheese and ham stuffing takes about 10 minutes and deep-frying 10-15 minutes.

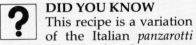

SERVING IDEAS
Serve with a salad of thinly sliced Mozzarella cheese and tomato, sprinkled with a little olive oil, seasoning and extra chopped herbs.

VARIATION
If fresh basil is not available use an extra tablespoon of chopped parsley.

DID YOU KNOW
This recipe is a variation of the Italian *panzarotti alla Romana*. The dough is a type of simple pasta. The Italians often use pasta in this way as a sort of batter.

● 70 calories per ravioli

70

Mustard chicken livers

SERVES 4
¾ lb chicken livers, cut into 1-inch pieces (see Preparation and Cook's tip)
2 tablespoons butter
1 large onion, roughly chopped
2 tablespoons grainy-style mustard
¼ teaspoon prepared English mustard
¼ cup thin cream
salt and freshly ground black pepper
3 scallions, sliced

SAVORY NOODLES
6 oz tagliatelle
1 tablespoon corn oil
1 cup chopped walnuts
2 tomatoes, diced

1 Melt the butter in a saucepan, add the onion and sauté gently for 5 minutes until limp. Add chicken livers and continue cooking for 10 minutes, stirring frequently.

Cook's Notes

 TIME
15 minutes preparation; 20 minutes cooking.

 COOK'S TIP
Frozen chicken livers may be used, but they must be thawed and drained thoroughly first.

 VARIATIONS
Lamb kidneys are also suitable for this recipe: cut in half and remove the center cores. Allow 2 or 3 more minutes cooking time at stage 3.
  Instead of tagliatelle, use pasta shapes or long-grain rice.

 PREPARATION
Remove gall bladders from the livers:

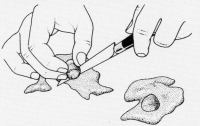

If pierced, their bitter fluid taints the flesh. Cut out with a small section of liver around and trim any green-tinged flesh.

●445 calories per portion

2 Meanwhile, bring a pan of salted water to a boil and cook the tagliatelle for 8-10 minutes until soft but still firm to the bite.
3 Add the mustards and cream to the chicken livers and season to taste with salt and black pepper. Continue cooking very gently for 5 minutes more, stirring occasionally.

4 Drain the tagliatelle thoroughly and put it into a bowl. Immediately add the oil, walnuts and tomatoes and mix together thoroughly.
5 Spoon the tagliatelle mixture on to warmed serving plates. Sprinkle over the scallions, then spoon the chicken liver mixture on top. Serve at once, while still hot.

71

Tangy fish sticks

SERVES 4
12 fish sticks
2 tablespoons cornstarch
1½ cups chicken broth
1 can (about ½ lb) pineapple pieces
 (see Buying guide)
2 tablespoons soy sauce
pinch of ground ginger
2 teaspoons tomato paste
2 tablespoons soft brown sugar
1 tablespoon vinegar
salt and freshly ground black
 pepper
½ red pepper, seeded and diced
4 scallions, chopped
1 tablespoon vegetable oil
1 cup long-grain rice
2½ cups boiling water

1 teaspoon dried mixed herbs

1 In a saucepan, blend the cornstarch with a little broth to make a smooth paste, then gradually stir in the remaining broth.
2 Add the pineapple pieces, with their juice, to the saucepan with the soy sauce, ginger, tomato paste, sugar and vinegar and season to taste with salt and pepper.
3 Add the red pepper and scallions to the pan and bring to a boil, stirring. Lower the heat, cover the pan and leave to simmer, stirring occasionally while cooking the rice, (see stage 4).
4 Heat the broiler to medium. Heat the oil in a large saucepan over low heat, add the rice and stir to coat the grains thoroughly. Pour in the boiling water (see Cook's tips) add the herbs and stir once. Bring to a boil, then simmer, covered, for about 15 minutes, until the rice is tender and the cooking liquid is all absorbed.
5 While the rice is cooking, broil the fish sticks for 8-10 minutes, turning once, until golden on both sides. Cut each fish stick into 3-4 bite-sized pieces.
6 Divide the rice between 4 warmed plates.
7 Place the fish stick pieces on top of the rice, dividing them equally between the portions. Spoon the hot sauce over each portion and serve at once.

Cook's Notes

TIME
Preparation and cooking take about 35 minutes, including the rice.

FOR CHILDREN
Children will enjoy this dish, although the red pepper is perhaps best omitted if serving to very young children and toddlers.

VARIATIONS
Instead of using fish sticks, stir a cup of roughly chopped cooking pork into the sauce before serving with the rice.

BUYING GUIDE
Canned pineapple pieces are less expensive than chunks or rings. If they are not available, buy pineapple chunks, chop them and use in the same way.

WATCHPOINT
Remove pan from heat as soon as the rice is cooked, so that it does not stick.

COOK'S TIPS
Coating the rice grains with oil ensures that they stay separate during cooking.
 Simmering the rice in twice its volume of boiling water, which is absorbed by the end of cooking, gives a really fluffy result.

●490 calories per portion

72

Kabanos fiesta

SERVES 4
2 tablespoons vegetable oil
1 onion, finely chopped
1 small green pepper, seeded and
  finely chopped
1 can (about 1 lb) tomatoes
1 teaspoon paprika
½ teaspoon sugar
salt and freshly ground black
  pepper
6 oz kabanos sausages, cut into
  ½ inch slices (see Buying guide)
1½ cups cooked long-grain rice (see
  Cook's tip)
2 tablespoons chopped parsley, for
  garnish

1 Heat the oil in a saucepan and sauté the onion and pepper over medium heat until limp.
2 Add the tomatoes and their juice, paprika, sugar, and salt and pepper to taste. Bring to a boil, breaking up the tomatoes with a wooden spoon. Lower the heat and simmer, uncovered, for 10 minutes, stirring from time to time.
3 Add the kabanos and rice to the sauce, stir well and simmer for a further 5 minutes or so.
4 Serve immediately in a warmed serving dish, garnished with the chopped parsley.

Cook's Notes

TIME
Preparing and cooking take 30 minutes.

BUYING GUIDE
Kabanos, a Polish pork sausage, is available in delicatessens – 2 sausages should provide the amount needed. If unavailable, use some pepperoni or chorizos.

COOK'S TIP
This is a good way of using up left-over rice. If using raw rice, cook ½ cup long-grain rice in cup boiling water or broth.

●375 calories per portion

Sauces for a pasta party

With fresh pasta now so widely available at delicatessens and supermarkets, an easy way to entertain friends is to hold a pasta party. The sauces given below combine perfectly with any type of fresh pasta. All you need to serve with them is a green salad tossed in a well-flavored dressing and some Italian wine. Prepare the sauces in advance and then cook the pasta once your friends have arrived.

For this menu, buy plain white pasta made with egg, or green or wholemeal pasta. Choose tagliatelle or spaghetti, and allow about ¼ lb per person. Alternatively, make your own pasta with a pasta machine (available from specialist kitchen stores and large department stores) – just follow manufacturer's instructions.

To cook 1 lb fresh pasta, add about 1 tablespoon salt to a large saucepan of water, then bring to a boil. Add the pasta, bring back to a boil, then lower the heat slightly, stir once and simmer for about 3 minutes until *al dente* (tender, yet firm to the bite). Drain in a colander and serve at once with the sauce separately.

Gorgonzola sauce

SERVES 4-6
¼ lb Gorgonzola cheese, cut into small pieces (see Buying guide)
½ cup milk
¼ cup butter
¼ cup heavy cream
freshly ground black pepper
finely chopped parsley, for garnish

COUNTDOWN
The day before
●Make the Gorgonzola sauce up to the end of stage 1. Cool, then cover closely with plastic wrap and refrigerate.
●Make the Pesto up to the end of stage 2, then cover and refrigerate.
●Make the Ham provençal sauce, then cover and refrigerate.

1 Pour the milk into a heavy-bottomed saucepan and heat gently until hot but not simmering. Add the cheese and butter and stir gently with a wooden spoon until smooth.
2 Add the cream to the pan with pepper to taste and heat through gently. Do not allow the sauce to simmer. Serve at once, straight from the pan.

Pesto

SERVES 4-6
1 cup fresh basil leaves
½ cup chopped fresh parsley
3 tablespoons pignoli
2 cloves garlic
1 cup olive oil
½ cup grated Parmesan cheese
¼ cup butter, softened and cut into small pieces
¼ teaspoon sugar
¼ teaspoon salt
freshly ground black pepper
1 tablespoon pasta cooking water

1 Put the basil, parsley, pignoli and garlic in a blender or food processor and work until finely chopped.
2 With machine running, slowly pour in the olive oil, then add the Parmesan cheese followed by the butter, sugar and salt. Season to taste with pepper, then transfer to a

2 hours before
●Make the salad.
5 minutes before
●Cook the pasta.
●Add the cream to the Gorgonzola sauce and heat through.
●Reheat the Ham provençal sauce.
Just before serving
●Stir 1 tablespoon of the pasta water into the Pesto.

pan or bowl (see Storage).
3 Just before serving, add the tablespoon of pasta cooking water, stir well and serve at once.

Ham provençal sauce

SERVES 4-6
1 tablespoon butter
1 tablespoon olive oil
¼ lb pancetta bacon, finely diced (see Buying guide)
1 onion, sliced
1 clove garlic, thinly sliced (optional)
1 can (about 1½ lb) tomatoes
1 tablespoon tomato paste
1 teaspoon Italian herb seasoning or dried mixed herbs
½ teaspoon freshly ground black pepper
salt

1 Melt the butter in the oil in a large skillet. Add the bacon and sauté for 2 minutes. Add the onion and garlic, if using, and sauté for 3 minutes more until limp.
2 Stir in the tomatoes and their juice, tomato paste, herb seasoning and pepper. Bring to a boil, then lower the heat, cover the pan and simmer for 20 minutes. Season to taste with salt and serve the sauce at once, straight from the pan.

Cook's Notes

Gorgonzola sauce

TIME
This sauce takes just 10 minutes to make.

BUYING GUIDE
Gorgonzola is an Italian blue-veined cheese, with a strong flavor and a creamy texture which melts easily. Italian Dolcelatte cheese can be used with the same results, but the flavor will be considerably milder.

●270 calories per portion

Pesto

TIME
This sauce takes about 5 minutes to make in a blender or food processor.

STORAGE
Covered tightly, pesto can be kept in the refrigerator for about 1 week.

DID YOU KNOW
Pesto is the famous basil sauce from the port of Genoa in northern Italy, where basil grows prolifically. It is used there mostly as a sauce for pasta and as a flavoring for soups.

For an authentic flavor, it is most important to use fresh basil and grated fresh Parmesan cheese – the latter is available from most delicatessens and some large supermarkets.

●680 calories per portion

Ham provençal sauce

TIME
10 minutes preparation, 20 minutes cooking.

BUYING GUIDE
Pancetta is an Italian raw, fatty bacon with a distinctive, sweetish flavor. It is available from most good delicatessens and Italian food stores. As an alternative, used smoked ordinary bacon.

SERVING IDEAS
Serve with topping of grated Parmesan.

●160 calories per portion

Vegetables in curry sauce

SERVES 4
1 small cauliflower, divided into flowerets
½ lb small carrots, scraped and thickly sliced
½ lb green beans, trimmed and cut into chunks
½ lb shelled lima beans
salt

SAUCE
2 tablespoons butter
¼ cup all-purpose flour
1 tablespoon mild curry powder
large pinch of ground ginger
1¼ cups milk
2 tablespoons fresh orange juice
freshly ground black pepper
2 tablespoons thin cream or half and half
1 tablespoon blanched almonds, halved
1 tablespoon chopped mint or parsley

1 Cook all the prepared vegetables together in boiling salted water until they are just tender – no more than 10 minutes. Do not allow them to become limp. Drain the vegetables, reserving the broth, and put them on a serving dish. Keep hot.
2 To make the sauce: melt the butter in a saucepan, add the flour and stir to form a smooth paste, or roux. Stir in the curry powder and ginger and stir over medium heat for 3 minutes.
3 Gradually pour on the milk, orange juice and 1¼ cups of the reserved broth, still stirring. Bring to a boil and simmer for 3 minutes. Taste the sauce and season with pepper, and salt if necessary. Remove the pan from the heat and stir in the cream.
4 Pour the sauce over the vegetables, lightly tossing them with a fork to coat them. Scatter with the almonds and chopped mint or parsley and serve on a bed of rice.

Cook's Notes

TIME
The preparation of the vegetables will take about 10 minutes, and the cooking of the vegetables and sauce about 25 minutes altogether.

FREEZING
Use 1 tablespoon cornstarch in place of flour if you wish to freeze the sauce. It is best to freeze the vegetables and sauce separately.

COOK'S TIPS
To blanch almonds: boil for 30 seconds, then pinch off the skins.

● 240 calories per portion

Fresh tomato sauce

MAKES ABOUT 2½ CUPS
1½ lb tomatoes, chopped (see
 Economy)
1 tablespoon butter or margarine
1 tablespoon vegetable oil
2 onions, chopped
2 tablespoons tomato paste
1 teaspoon sugar
1 teaspoon salt
1 tablespoon chopped fresh parsley
½ teaspoon chopped fresh basil,
 or ¼ teaspoon dried basil
freshly ground black pepper

1 Melt the butter in the oil in a saucepan, add the onions and sauté gently for 5 minutes until limp and lightly colored.

2 Add the tomatoes and tomato paste, sugar, salt, parsley, basil and pepper to taste. Stir well, cover and let simmer gently for about 20 minutes until tomatoes are very soft and mushy. Remove from the heat and leave for about 10 minutes to cool slightly.

3 Pour the mixture into the goblet of a blender and work until smooth, then press through a strainer to remove tomato skins (alternatively, if you do not have a blender, work the sauce mixture through a strainer to purée it).

4 Return the tomato sauce to the rinsed-out pan and reheat gently. Taste and adjust seasoning, if necessary, then serve as required (see Serving ideas).

Lamb kidneys in paprika sauce

SERVES 4

10 large lamb kidneys, skinned and halved
1 tablespoon butter or margarine
3 tablespoons vegetable oil
1 onion, finely chopped
2 carrots, coarsely grated
¼ cup all-purpose flour
1¼ cups chicken broth
1 tablespoon tomato paste
1-2 tablespoons paprika, according to taste
salt and freshly ground black pepper

Cook's Notes

TIME
Total preparation and cooking time is 45 minutes.

WATCHPOINT
Boiling or overcooking the kidneys stage 2 will toughen them.

SERVING IDEAS
Cook 2 cups pasta shapes, drain well and toss with 1 tablespoon finely chopped parsley. Arrange in a border around a hot serving dish and pour the prepared kidneys and sauce into the center. Sprinkle with a little paprika pepper.

FREEZING
Transfer the kidneys and sauce to a rigid container, cool quickly, then seal, label and freeze for up to 2 months. To serve: reheat gently from frozen in a heavy-bottomed saucepan, until bubbling. Stir frequently, adding a little water if the kidneys stick to the bottom of the pan.

●315 calories per portion

1 Remove the membrane and core from the kidneys, using kitchen scissors. Wash the kidneys and pat dry on kitchen paper, then cut each half into 4 pieces.

2 Melt the butter in 1 tablespoon of the oil in a medium saucepan or flameproof casserole, add the kidneys. Cook over high heat for about 5 minutes until they stiffen and turn color, stirring to prevent sticking. Transfer to a bowl together with the juices and set aside.

3 Lower the heat to medium, heat the remaining oil in the pan, then add the onion and sauté gently for 5 minutes until limp and lightly colored. Add the carrots and sauté for 3-4 minutes until just tender, then sprinkle in the flour and continue cooking for 1 minute, stirring.

4 Gradually stir in the chicken broth, with the tomato paste, 1 tablespoon paprika and salt and pepper to taste. Bring to a boil. Simmer for 1 minute, stirring constantly.

5 Add the kidneys to the sauce, cover and cook very gently for 5 minutes or until tender. Taste and add more paprika if wished. Transfer to a warmed serving dish and serve (see Serving ideas).

Spaghetti with herby sauce

SERVES 4
1 lb spaghetti
2 tablespoons olive oil
1 medium onion, chopped
1 clove garlic, crushed (optional)
1 green pepper, seeded and chopped
¼ lb mushrooms, sliced
2 cans (1 lb each) tomatoes
salt and freshly ground black pepper
2 tablespoons butter or margarine
⅓ cup Parmesan cheese, grated
2 teaspoons Italian seasoning (see Did you know)

1 Heat the oil in a saucepan, add the onion, garlic, if using, green pepper and mushrooms and stir over medium heat for about 10 minutes until softened.

2 Stir the tomatoes with their juice into the softened vegetables, breaking them up with a wooden spoon, and bring to a boil. Lower the heat, add salt and pepper to taste, then simmer for 20 minutes, stirring occasionally.

3 Meanwhile, cook the spaghetti in a large pan of boiling salted water for 10-12 minutes or until *al dente* (tender, yet firm to the bite).

4 Drain the spaghetti thoroughly, then return to the rinsed-out pan. Add the butter, half the Parmesan, the Italian seasoning and salt and pepper to taste. Toss quickly until all the strands of spaghetti are coated, then transfer to a warmed serving dish.

5 Taste and adjust the seasoning of the herby sauce, then immediately pour over the spaghetti and mix well. Sprinkle with the remaining Parmesan and serve at once. Pass the sauce separately if you prefer.

Cook's Notes

TIME
Preparation of this dish is 15 minutes; cooking time about 25 minutes.

DID YOU KNOW
Italian seasoning is a brand of dried mixed herbs composed of oregano, thyme, parsley, sweet basil, pepper and bay leaves. It is available at supermarkets but, if not, make your own herb mixture to suit your taste.

VARIATION
Drain the tomatoes before adding to the vegetables and replace the tomato juice with ½ cup red wine.

●685 calories per portion

Sweetbreads in tomato sauce

SERVES 4
1½ lb lamb sweetbreads
salt
6 tablespoons butter or margarine
2 shallots, finely chopped
1 lb tomatoes, chopped
1 teaspoon freshly chopped
    tarragon, or ½ teaspoon dried
    tarragon
freshly ground black pepper

MARINADE
¼ cup lemon juice
1 tablespoon vegetable oil
2 tablespoons chopped parsley

TO SERVE
freshly cooked tagliatelle

1 Soak the sweetbreads in salted water for about 3½ hours, changing the water occasionally, until they turn white.
2 Meanwhile melt 2 tablespoons butter over medium heat and cook the shallots until they are limp and transparent. Stir in the tomatoes and cook over very low heat for 10 minutes. Remove from the heat and leave to cool slightly, then work in a blender and sieve to remove tomato skins. If you do not have a blender just press the mixture through a sieve. Stir in the tarragon and salt and pepper to taste. Set aside.
3 Drain the sweetbreads, then rinse them under cold running water. Blanch them by placing in a saucepan of fresh, salted water and bringing quickly to a boil. Lower the heat and simmer for 3 minutes.
4 Drain and rinse the sweetbreads again, then peel away the skin and remove any stringy tissue and gristle. Set aside.
5 To make the marinade: mix together the lemon juice, oil, parsley and salt and pepper to taste. Place the sweetbreads in a bowl, then pour over the marinade. Mix well and leave for 30 minutes.
6 Drain the sweetbreads on kitchen paper, pressing them firmly to flatten them and extract as much moisture as possible. Wipe dry, then slice thinly. Melt the remaining butter in a skillet, add the sweetbreads and sauté for 10-15 minutes until tender and lightly browned. Meanwhile, reheat the tomato sauce, and adjust seasoning.
7 Put freshly cooked tagliatelle in a serving dish and spoon the sweetbread and sauce into the center.

TIME
15 minutes cooking, but allow about 4 hours for soaking the sweetbreads in water and preparing them for cooking.

SERVING IDEAS
Serve on a bed of fresh tagliatelle, with a crisp salad of Chinese cabbage.

VARIATIONS
Use dry white wine instead of the lemon juice in the marinade, and if you do not want to go to the trouble of making the tomato sauce, simply sauté the sweetbreads and serve instead with canned tomato or tartar sauce.
Replace ¼ lb sweetbreads with 4 smoked bacon slices, roughly chopped. Sauté the bacon with the sweetbreads.
Before cooking the sweetbreads, dip them in beaten egg and bread crumbs.

●375 calories per portion

Tagliatelle with sorrel sauce

SERVES 4
¼ lb sorrel (see Buying guide)
2 tablespoons butter
½ cup chicken broth
1 tablespoon all-purpose flour
½ cup heavy double cream
freshly ground black pepper
little freshly grated nutmeg
salt
1 lb fresh tagliatelle
finely snipped chives, for garnish

1 Wash the sorrel well and remove any thick stalks. Dry the sorrel in a salad spinner, or leave to drain in a colander until dry.
2 Melt half the butter in a saucepan, add the sorrel leaves and stir over medium heat for 4-5 minutes, until the sorrel is completely soft and reduced to a small mass.
3 Put the sorrel in a blender with the broth and blend until smooth.

4 Melt the remaining butter in the rinsed-out saucepan, sprinkle in the flour and stir over low heat for 1-2 minutes until straw-colored. Gradually stir in sorrel and broth mixture and simmer, stirring, until smooth and well combined.
5 Remove from the heat, then stir in the cream and season to taste with pepper and nutmeg. Heat through without boiling.

6 Meanwhile, bring a large pan of salted water to a boil and cook the fresh tagliatelle for 5 minutes or until it is just tender but still firm to the bite (*al dente*).
7 Drain the pasta well, then return to the pan, pour the sauce over and toss until the pasta is evenly coated. Transfer to a warmed serving dish, sprinkle with snipped chives and serve at once.

Cook's Notes

 TIME
Only about 20 minutes to prepare the sauce and cook the fresh pasta.

 BUYING GUIDE
Sorrel is not always available in stores, but it is easy to grow from seed in the garden for harvesting in summer. If unobtainable, fresh spinach or watercress may be used as a substitute.

 SERVING IDEAS
Sorrel sauce has a very subtle flavor which enhances mild-flavored foods. Try it poured over fish kabobs or fish steaks, veal scollops, poached eggs or a plain French omelet. This dish could be served as an appetizer followed by a light main course, or as a tasty snack at any time.

●660 calories per portion

Peas portugaise

SERVES 4
1 lb frozen peas
2 tablespoons vegetable oil
1 medium onion, finely chopped
1 clove garlic, crushed (optional)
2 teaspoons paprika
1 can (about 14 oz) tomatoes (see Variation)
1 teaspoon caster sugar
celery salt and freshly ground black pepper

1 Heat the oil in a saucepan, add the onion and garlic, if using, and sauté over medium heat for 3-4 minutes, stirring occasionally, until the onion is limp but not colored. Stir in the paprika and cook for 2 minutes more, then stir in the tomatoes with their juice, the sugar, celery salt and pepper to taste.

Bring to a boil, lower the heat and simmer uncovered, for about 10 minutes until the tomato sauce is reduced to a thick purée.

2 Meanwhile, cook the peas in a small quantity of boiling salted water, according to package directions. Drain well.

3 Turn the peas into a warmed serving dish. Taste and adjust the seasoning of the tomato sauce, then spoon it over the peas and fork through lightly so that the sauce can run through the peas to flavor them. Serve the peas at once, while very hot (see Serving ideas).

Sweet and sour sauce

SERVES 4
¾ lb wholemeal spaghetti (see
  Cook's tips)
⅓ cup grated Parmesan cheese, to
  serve

SWEET AND SOUR SAUCE
1½ lb tomatoes, peeled and
  roughly chopped
2 tablespoons butter
2 tablespoons olive or vegetable oil
2 onions, roughly chopped
1 clove garlic, crushed (optional)
1 cup vegetable bouillon (see
  Buying guide)
½ cup currants
2 teaspoons wine vinegar
1 teaspoon sugar
1 bay leaf
½ teaspoon dried basil
½ teaspoon dried thyme
¼ teaspoon ground cinnamon
salt and ground black pepper

Cook's Notes

 TIME
Preparation and cooking
takes 1¼ hours.

 COOK'S TIPS
Wholemeal spaghetti
has a mild, nutty flavor
and a higher fiber content than
ordinary spaghetti. The tangy
sauce can be made in advance
and reheated just before
serving.

 BUYING GUIDE
Vegetable bouillon
cubes are available from
health food shops and delicatessens. However, if they are
difficult to obtain, use chicken
bouillon cubes instead. Alternatively, use the liquid saved from
cooking vegetables or use red
wine instead of broth and omit
the sugar from the sauce.

●505 calories per portion

1 Make the sauce: melt the butter in
the oil in a large saucepan, add the
onions and sauté gently for 5 minutes until limp and lightly colored.
2 Add the remaining sauce ingredients with salt and pepper to taste.
Bring to a boil then lower the heat
and simmer, uncovered, for 40-50
minutes, until thick, stirring occasionally and breaking up the tomato
pieces with a wooden spoon (see
Cook's tips).

3 Bring a large pan of salted water
to a boil and cook the spaghetti for
15-20 minutes or until tender, yet
firm to the bite. Drain the spaghetti
very thoroughly in a colander or
strainer.
4 Divide the spaghetti between 4
warmed individual serving plates or
shallow soup bowls and spoon over
the hot sauce. Serve at once, with
the grated Parmesan cheese passed
separately in a small bowl.

VEGETABLES AND SALADS

Stuffed green peppers

SERVES 4
4 green peppers (see Buying guide)
½ cup long-grain rice
1 small onion, chopped
3 tablespoons vegetable oil
2 tablespoons tomato paste
5 tablespoons water
½ cup sliced flaked almonds
⅓ cup golden raisins
2 teaspoons dried oregano
grated rind of 1 orange
salt and freshly ground black
pepper

1 Preheat oven to 350°.
2 Bring a large saucepan of water to a boil, add the rice, bring back to a boil, then lower the heat and cook for about 15 minutes until the rice is tender.
3 Slice the tops off the peppers and reserve them. Carefully remove the seeds from the peppers.
4 Drain the rice, rinse under cold running water and drain again.
5 In a bowl, thoroughly mix the rice together with all the remaining ingredients, reserving 2 tablespoons of the oil and 2 tablespoons of the water.
6 Fill the peppers with the stuffing mixture, packing it in well but taking care not to break the peppers.
7 Put the peppers into a casserole in which they will stand together closely but comfortably (see Cook's tip). Replace the tops.
8 Mix together the reserved oil and water. Drizzle it over the peppers.

9 Cover the dish and bake for 25 minutes. Uncover for a further 25 minutes. Serve hot, warm or cold.

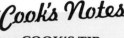
Cook's Notes

 TIME
Preparation takes about 30 minutes, including cooking the rice. Cooking in the oven takes 50 minutes.

 BUYING GUIDE
Buy firm, squat peppers as they stand up better in the dish and the stuffing will not fall out.

COOK'S TIP
If necessary, put a little crumpled foil between the peppers to keep them upright. Do not forget to remove it before serving.

 VARIATION
Red peppers could be used instead of green or use 2 of each.

SERVING IDEAS
These make a tasty supper dish on their own or with a tomato sauce, served with hot garlic or peda bread. They are especially good served warm. They could be served as a hearty appetizer, before a fairly light main course.

●325 calories per portion

84

Creamy rich rigatoni

SERVES 4
1 lb rigatoni (see Buying guide)
salt
1 tablespoon vegetable oil
$\frac{2}{3}$ cup butter
$\frac{1}{4}$ lb button mushrooms, sliced
$\frac{1}{2}$ cup thin single cream
2 egg yolks
$\frac{1}{2}$ cup grated Parmesan cheese
pinch of freshly grated nutmeg
freshly ground black pepper
$\frac{1}{2}$ cup frozen peas, cooked

1 Bring a large saucepan of salted water to a boil. Add the rigatoni and oil, lower the heat and simmer for about 12 minutes until just tender but still firm to the bité.
2 Meanwhile, melt 2 tablespoons butter in a skillet. Add the mushrooms and sauté over medium heat until they have softened and are just tender. Set aside.
3 Make the sauce: melt the remaining butter in a large saucepan. Remove from the heat and set aside. In a bowl, quickly mix the cream, egg yolks and Parmesan with the nutmeg. Season with salt and plenty of pepper. Add this mixture to the melted butter in the pan and stir well.
4 When the rigatoni is nearly cooked, set the saucepan with the sauce mixture over very low heat to warm it through slightly, stirring gently all the time.
5 Drain the cooked rigatoni, add to the cream sauce with the peas and the mushrooms and stir constantly for a few seconds, then pile into warmed individual serving dishes and serve at once.

Cook's Notes

 TIME
Preparation time is about 10 minutes, total cooking time 15 minutes.

WATCHPOINT
When heating the cream mixture, watch it very carefully so that the eggs do not begin to scramble.

 SERVING IDEAS
Serve as a supper or lunch dish with a tossed green salad. Offer extra Parmesan for sprinkling over the pasta if you like.

 BUYING GUIDE
Rigatoni, a pasta that looks like large, ribbed macaroni, is available from delicatessens and some supermarkets. If it is difficult to obtain, use ordinary elbow macaroni instead.

●870 calories per portion

Noodles Chinese-style

SERVES 4
¼ lb Chinese egg noodles (see Buying guide)
salt
2 tablespoons vegetable oil
6 scallions, sliced
1 tablespoon grated fresh gingerroot
1 lb Chinese cabbage, cut into ½-inch thick slices
¾ cup diced lean cooked ham (see Economy)
¼ lb bean sprouts
1 tablespoon soy sauce (see Buying guide)
¼ cup chicken broth, dry sherry or water
freshly ground black pepper

1 Bring a large saucepan of salted water to a boil. Add the noodles, bring back to a boil and cook for about 3 minutes or according to package instructions, until just tender. Drain and set aside.

Cook's Notes

TIME
10 minutes preparation, 10 minutes cooking.

ECONOMY
Any left-over lean cooked meat can be substituted for the ham.

SERVING IDEAS
This Chinese-style dish is particularly good served as a vegetable accompaniment to broiled or fried fish, chops or chicken.

To serve as a quick, economical light lunch or supper dish, double the quantities. If liked, add extra ingredients such as sliced mushrooms or cooked shelled shrimp.

BUYING GUIDE
Thin Chinese egg noodles are available at supermarkets and delicatessens, but if difficult to obtain, Italian spaghetti or egg noodles can be used instead. These will need longer initial cooking in water – follow package instructions.

Some supermarkets may have a choice of soy sauces - choose the lighter type for this dish.

●230 calories per portion

2 Heat the oil in a wok or large skillet, add the scallions and ginger and sauté for 2 minutes, stirring.
3 Add the Chinese cabbage to the pan with the diced ham. Sauté for 2 minutes more.
4 Add the drained noodles, together with the bean sprouts, soy sauce, broth and salt and pepper to taste. Increase the heat to medium and stir-fry for about 5 minutes until the vegetables are tender but still crisp and most of the liquid in the pan has evaporated.
5 Taste and adjust seasoning. Turn into a warmed serving dish.

Vegetable lasagne

SERVES 4
¾ lb plain lasagne
2 tablespoons plus 1 teaspoon
    vegetable oil
2 onions, sliced
1 green pepper, seeded and sliced
½ lb zucchini, sliced
½ lb mushrooms, sliced
1 can (about 1 lb) tomatoes
1 teaspoon dried mixed herbs
1 clove garlic, crushed (optional)
salt and freshly ground black
    pepper
3 tablespoons tomato paste
melted margarine, for greasing
1 fresh tomato, sliced

CHEESE SAUCE
¼ cup butter or margarine
½ cup all-purpose flour
2½ cups warm milk
2 cups grated Cheddar cheese

1 Heat 2 tablespoons oil in a large heavy-bottomed saucepan. Add the onions and sauté over medium heat for about 10 minutes until limp.

2 Add the green pepper and sauté for another 2-3 minutes, then add the zucchini, mushrooms, tomatoes and their juice, herbs and garlic, if using. Add salt and pepper to taste, stir well, then simmer, uncovered, for 15 minutes, until vegetables are tender, stirring occasionally.

3 Stir in the tomato paste and cook for 15 minutes more until the liquid has reduced and the mixture is thick. Taste and adjust seasoning.

4 Meanwhile, cook the lasagne: pour about 3 quarts salted water into a very large saucepan with 1 teaspoon oil and bring to a boil. Add the lasagne a piece at a time and boil rapidly, uncovered, for 15-20 minutes until just tender, stirring frequently. Drain, rinse under cold running water, then leave to drain on kitchen paper.

5 Preheat oven to 400°. Grease a 2-quart flameproof dish or casserole with melted margarine.

6 Make the cheese sauce: melt the margarine in a small saucepan, sprinkle in the flour and stir over low heat for 1-2 minutes until straw-colored. Remove from the heat and gradually stir in the milk. Return to the heat and simmer, stirring, until thick and smooth. Stir in half the cheese, and season to taste.

7 Arrange the vegetable mixture, lasagne and cheese sauce in layers in the prepared dish, starting with the vegetable mixture and ending with cheese sauce. Sprinkle over the remaining cheese, top with tomato slices, and bake for 45 minutes until golden. Blot off excess oil with kitchen paper. Serve hot.

Cook's Notes

 TIME
Preparation 45 minutes, cooking 45 minutes.

WATCHPOINTS
To add the lasagne to the boiling water, either bend it carefully or, if it is in long pieces, break them in half. The addition of the oil, and frequent stirring, are essential to prevent the strips sticking together.

FREEZING
Open freeze, turn out and foil wrap. Store for up to 3 months. To serve: bake from frozen in the original dish, allowing an extra 15-20 minutes cooking time.

 SERVING IDEAS
Serve for lunch or supper with a salad of endive, corn kernels and watercress tossed in French dressing.

●935 calories per portion

Eggplant and pasta bake

SERVES 4

2 cans (about 1 lb) eggplant in sunflower seed oil (see Buying guide)
2 tablespoons vegetable oil
1 large onion, chopped
1 red pepper, seeded and chopped
1 teaspoon dried mixed herbs
large pinch of ground cinnamon (see Cook's tips)
salt and freshly ground black pepper
1½ cups wholemeal elbow macaroni (see Variation)

TOPPING
2 eggs
½ cup plain yogurt
½ cup grated Cheddar cheese
paprika, for sprinkling

1 Preheat oven to 400°.
2 Heat the oil in a heavy-bottomed saucepan. Add the onion and red pepper and cook gently, stirring frequently, for about 10 minutes until the vegetables are softened. Stir in the eggplant and their oil, herbs, cinnamon and salt and pepper to taste. Remove from the heat, cover and keep warm.
3 While the vegetables are cooking, bring a large pan of salted water to a boil. Add the macaroni and stir once. Bring the water back to a boil and cook for 9-11 minutes, until the macaroni is just tender, but still firm to the bite.
4 Drain the macaroni thoroughly, then stir into the eggplant mixture. Check the seasoning, then turn into a 2-quart flameproof baking or gratin dish and level the surface.
5 Make the topping: beat the eggs into the yogurt, then stir in the cheese and salt and pepper to taste. Pour over the eggplant mixture and sprinkle with paprika according to taste.
6 Bake in the oven for about 40 minutes, until the topping is set and browned (see Cook's tips). Serve hot, straight from the casserole.

Cook's Notes

 TIME
30 minutes preparation, plus about 40 minutes baking time.

 BUYING GUIDE
Canned eggplant, available in delicatessens and large supermarkets, are a useful buy when the fresh ones are not available.

● 700 calories per portion

 VARIATION
Use white macaroni instead of wholemeal but remember that it needs less time to cook.

 COOK'S TIPS
Cinnamon adds a hint of spice to the mixture, without making it 'sweet'.
The casserole can be left in the oven, with heat turned off, for 20-30 minutes without spoiling.

Chinese lettuce parcels

SERVES 6

6 large crisp lettuce leaves (see Preparation)
2 tablespoons vegetable oil
4 scallions, finely chopped
1 teaspoon ground ginger
1 celery stalk, finely chopped
⅔ cup finely chopped mushrooms
½ cup canned water chestnuts, drained and finely sliced
1 cup cooked long-grain rice
1 cup frozen peas, cooked and drained
1½ tablespoons soy sauce
1 egg, beaten
extra soy sauce, to serve

1 Heat the oil in a wok or large skillet. Add the scallions and ginger and sauté gently for 2-3 minutes until limp.
2 Add the celery, mushrooms and water chestnuts and sauté for a further 5 minutes.
3 Stir in the rice, peas and soy sauce. Remove the pan from the heat and stir in the egg.
4 Lay the lettuce leaves out flat on a work surface. Put about 2 generous tablespoons of the mixture at the base of each lettuce leaf. Fold the leaf around the mixture and roll up to form neat parcels. Secure with wooden picks, if necessary.
5 Place the parcels in a steamer. If you do not have a steamer, use a metal colander which fits neatly inside a saucepan (the base must

not touch the water). Fill the pan with boiling water, place the parcels in the colander and place the colander in the pan. Cover with foil or lid of steamer and steam for 5 minutes.
6 Remove the wooden picks from the parcels, if using, then place the parcels on a warmed serving dish. Serve at once with extra soy sauce passed separately.

Cook's Notes

 TIME
Preparation takes 30 minutes and cooking the parcels takes 5 minutes.

 DID YOU KNOW
Water chestnuts are bulbs from China which are grown under water.

 PREPARATION
Soften the lettuce leaves by dipping in boiling water for 10 seconds. Drain on kitchen paper.

● 140 calories per portion

Hot beans and rice

SERVES 4-6
1 can (about 1 lb) red kidney beans, drained
1 cup long-grain rice
2 tablespoons vegetable oil
1 onion, finely chopped
1 clove garlic, crushed (optional)
1 red pepper, seeded and thinly sliced
1 green pepper, seeded and thinly sliced
2 celery stalks, finely chopped
2 large tomatoes, peeled, seeded and chopped
1 tablespoon paprika
1 teaspoon cayenne pepper
freshly ground black pepper
2½ cups water
salt
celery leaves, for garnish

1 Heat the oil in a heavy-bottomed saucepan, add the onion and garlic, if using, and sauté gently until limp and lightly colored.
2 Add the sliced red and green peppers and celery and sauté for 3 minutes more. Add the tomatoes, drained beans, rice, paprika, cayenne and black pepper. Stir and cook for a further minute. Pour in the water, stir the mixture well and bring to a boil.
3 Cover and simmer gently for 25 minutes until the rice is tender and all the liquid has been absorbed. Season to taste.
4 Spoon the mixture into a warmed serving dish, garnish with the celery leaves and serve the bean and rice salad at once.

Cook's Notes

 TIME
Preparation takes about 20 minutes, final cooking takes 25 minutes.

 SERVING IDEAS
This substantial dish goes particularly well with broiled or barbecued meat. To serve cold as a salad, let cool, then toss in a well-seasoned oil and vinegar dressing.

 VARIATION
Use 1 cup dried kidney beans instead of the canned type. Soak the beans overnight, then put them in a pan and cover with fresh water. Boil briskly for at least 10 minutes then simmer gently for 1½-2 hours. Drain and proceed with the recipe as above.

●395 calories per portion

Stuffed cabbage pie

SERVES 4-6
1 green cabbage, weighing about 2 lb
¾ cup long-grain rice
salt
1 tablespoon butter or margarine
1 onion, chopped
1 green apple, weighing about 5 oz
⅓ cup chopped, pitted dates
1 orange (see Preparation)
¾ cup grated Cheddar cheese
1 egg, beaten
freshly ground black pepper
margarine, for greasing

1 Preheat oven to 350° and grease a flameproof dish 8 inches in diameter and 3 inches deep.
2 Bring a pan of salted water to a boil and cook the rice for about 10 minutes until just tender, but still firm to the bite.
3 Meanwhile, remove about 8 outer leaves of the cabbage and cut off any thick hard midribs. Bring another pan of salted water to a boil and blanch the cabbage leaves for 4 minutes. Drain and set aside. Chop the remaining cabbage and put on one side.
4 Melt the butter in a large saucepan, add the onion and sauté gently for 5 minutes until limp.
5 Add the chopped cabbage to the pan and cook over medium heat, stirring, for 5 minutes. Pare, core and chop the apple and add to the pan. Cook for a minute more.
6 Drain the rice thoroughly and add to the pan with the dates, orange rind and juice. Remove from heat.
7 Line the bottom and sides of the dish with half the blanched cabbage leaves, arranging them so that they overlap and allowing them to overhang the dish. Stir the cheese and egg into the rice mixture, season to taste with salt and pepper, then spoon into the lined dish. Level the surface of the mixture and cover with the remaining leaves. Fold over overhanging leaves.
8 Cover the dish tightly with foil and cook for 45 minutes.
9 Loosen the sides with a knife and turn out on to a warmed plate.

Cook's Notes

 TIME
45 minutes preparation, including boiling the rice and blanching the leaves, then 45 minutes in the oven.

 PREPARATION
Grate the rind of half the orange and squeeze the juice from the whole orange.

●370 calories per portion

 SERVING IDEAS
Serve as an accompaniment to meat dishes, as an appetizer or as a complete vegetarian meal with a homemade tomato sauce poured over the top.

 VARIATION
Use soaked dried apricots or drained canned apricots instead of the dates.

91

Vegetable fried rice

SERVES 4
1 cup long-grain rice
salt
2 cups diced carrots
1 parsnip, diced
1 small turnip, diced
2 tablespoons vegetable oil
1 large onion, chopped
1 clove garlic, crushed (optional)
½ cup sliced button mushrooms
2 large tomatoes, peeled and sliced
½ cup frozen peas, thawed
freshly ground black pepper
2 eggs, lightly beaten
1 tablespoon chopped fresh parsley
grated Parmesan cheese, to serve

1 Bring a large saucepan of salted water to a boil, add the rice and cover. Lower the heat and simmer for 10 minutes, or until the rice is just tender, but still firm to the bite.
2 Meanwhile, bring another pan of salted water to a boil. Add the carrots, parsnip and turnip and cover. Lower the heat and cook for about 8-10 minutes, or until all the

vegetables are barely tender.
3 Drain the cooked root vegetables and reserve. Drain the rice in a strainer and rinse well under hot running water to separate the grains. Drain again.
4 Heat the oil in a large non-stick saucepan, add the onion and garlic, if using, and sauté gently for 5 minutes, until the onion is limp and lighty colored.
5 Add the drained root vegetables

to the pan, together with the mushrooms, tomatoes, peas and rice. Stir well and season to taste with salt and plenty of pepper. Cover the pan and cook over very low heat for 10 minutes.
6 Stir in the eggs and gently turn the mixture so that the egg cooks. Remove from the heat and turn into a warmed serving dish. Garnish with the parsley and serve at once with the Parmesan cheese.

Rice-stuffed zucchini

SERVES 4
4 zucchini
1 tablespoon vegetable oil
1 onion, finely chopped
½ lb chicken livers, chopped
¾ cup cooked long-grain rice (see Cook's tip)
2 tomatoes, chopped
2 tablespoons chopped parsley
pinch of thyme
1 teaspoon lemon juice
salt and freshly ground black pepper
green and red pepper rings
sprigs of fresh thyme and parsley and lemon twist, for garnish
margarine, for greasing

1 Preheat oven to 375°. Grease a flameproof dish.
2 Cut the zucchini in half lengthwise and scoop out the seeds. Arrange in a single layer in the prepared dish.

3 Make the stuffing: heat the oil in a saucepan. Add the onion and sauté gently for 5 minutes until limp and lightly colored. Add the chicken livers and cook for 5 minutes more, stirring, until evenly browned. Remove pan from heat.
4 Add rice, tomatoes, herbs and lemon juice and mix well. Season to

taste with salt and pepper.
5 Spoon the stuffing into each zucchini half, pressing it down firmly.
6 Cover the dish with greased foil and cook in the oven for 35-40 minutes, until the zucchini are tender. Serve hot on a bed of pepper rings, garnished with herbs and a lemon twist.

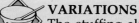
Cook's Notes

 TIME
Preparation takes about 25 minutes and cooking takes 35-40 minutes.

 SERVING IDEAS
Stuffed zucchini are very good on their own for a light lunch. Alternatively, for a more substantial dish serve with gravy or tomato sauce and mixed vegetables.

 COOK'S TIP
For this amount of cooked rice you will need ¼ cup raw rice.

VARIATIONS
The stuffing also makes a delicious filling for eggplant: cut a small eggplant in half and remove the seeds. Place the halves in a single layer in a flameproof dish and fill the center hollows with the stuffing.

Use turkey or lamb liver instead of chicken livers.

Alternatively, use lean cooked ham and replace the tomatoes with mushrooms.

● 190 calories per portion

Spinach and sage rice

SERVES 4
½ lb spinach, stalks and midribs removed, finely chopped (see Watchpoint)
2 tablespoons vegetable oil
1 small onion, finely chopped
1 tablespoon lemon juice
½ teaspoon powdered dried sage
1½ teaspoons salt
freshly ground black pepper
1 cup long-grain rice
2¼ cups boiling water
3 tablespoons grated cheese

1 Heat the oil in a medium saucepan and add the spinach, onion, lemon juice, sage, ½ teaspoon of the salt and plenty of freshly ground black pepper. Cook over medium heat for 5 minutes, stirring constantly until the spinach is soft and the mixture is fairly dry.
2 Lower the heat, add the rice to the pan and cook gently for a further 2 minutes, stirring. Pour in the boiling water, add the remaining salt and bring back to a boil. Stir once, then lower the heat, cover the pan and cook very gently for 20 minutes, until the rice is cooked and the liquid has been absorbed.
3 Stir the mixture, turn it into a warmed serving dish, sprinkle with cheese and serve at once as an accompaniment to meat dishes, particularly pork.

Cook's Notes

 TIME
20 minutes preparation, 30 minutes cooking.

WATCHPOINT
After washing the spinach it is important to dry it thoroughly, a leaf at a time, in a clean dish-towel, otherwise it will make the rice too wet and spoil the dish.

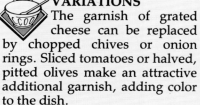 VARIATIONS
The garnish of grated cheese can be replaced by chopped chives or onion rings. Sliced tomatoes or halved, pitted olives make an attractive additional garnish, adding color to the dish.

●330 calories per portion

94

Chicken and pasta salad

SERVES 4
2 cups cooked chicken, cubed
1¼ cups pasta shells
salt
1 teaspoon vegetable oil
½ cup dairy sour cream
1 tablespoon capers
2 scallions, chopped
1 tablespoon chopped fresh
  tarragon (see Variations)
salt and freshly ground black
  pepper
a little extra chopped tarragon, for
  garnish

1 Bring a large pan of salted water to a boil, swirl in the oil, then add the pasta. Bring back to a boil and cook for 7-10 minutes until tender.
2 Drain thoroughly, then rinse under cold running water to remove excess starch (see Cook's tip).

Drain again and set aside until cold.
3 Mix all the other ingredients together thoroughly and stir in the pasta shells. Season. Turn into a deep serving bowl and garnish with tarragon. Serve cold.

Cook's Notes

TIME
Total preparation takes about 20 minutes.

SERVING IDEAS
Serve with a simple green or tomato salad.

COOK'S TIP
Rinsing the pasta under cold water also prevents it sticking together when cold.

VARIATIONS
If fresh tarragon is not available, use another fresh herb such as mint, parsley or chives.

For a more substantial dish, add a quartered hard-cooked egg per person.

Cold cooked fish may be used instead of cooked chicken.

●325 calories per portion

Pasta salad

SERVES 4
½ lb green tagliatelle
salt
1 can (1¾ oz) anchovy fillets,
  drained and soaked in milk for
  20 minutes
2 cups finely diced Cheddar cheese
2 tomatoes, peeled and thickly
  sliced
2 celery stalks, chopped
8 ripe olives, halved and pitted
2 tablespoons grated Parmesan
  cheese

DRESSING
3 tablespoons vegetable oil
1 tablespoon wine vinegar
½ teaspoon mustard powder
salt and freshly ground black
  pepper

1 Cook the tagliatelle in boiling salted water for 5-10 minutes until just tender. Drain thoroughly, then rinse well under cold running water, to remove any excess starch from the pasta.
2 While the pasta is cooking, make the dressing: combine the oil, vinegar, mustard and salt and pepper to taste in a screw-top jar. Shake the jar well until all the ingredients in the dressing are thoroughly blended.
3 Drain the anchovy fillets and pat dry with kitchen paper. Put in a bowl with cooked tagliatelle, cheese, tomatoes, celery, and olives, then pour in the dressing. Toss gently, until all the ingredients are evenly coated.
4 Pile the salad on to a serving dish and sprinkle the Parmesan cheese over the top.

Cook's Notes

TIME
This salad takes about 20 minutes; including the cooking of the tagliatelle.

SERVING IDEAS
Serve this tasty salad as a lunch or supper dish with a green salad and some hot garlic bread.

VARIATION
Other pasta shapes, such as shells or short tubes, can be used.

WATCHPOINT
It is very important not to overcook the pasta, or the salad with be starchy.

●600 calories per portion

96

Tropicana salad

SERVES 4-6
1 cup pasta shapes
2 grapefruits, peeled and sectioned
2 oranges, peeled and sectioned
2 large dessert apples, diced
3 celery stalks, finely chopped
¼ lb salami, skinned and roughly chopped
1 tablespoon snipped chives
¼ cup salted cashew nuts

DRESSING
4 tablespoons thick mayonnaise
2 tablespoons fresh orange juice
finely grated rind and juice of 1 lemon
salt and freshly ground black pepper

FOR GARNISH
slices of unpeeled orange
watercress

1 Bring a pan of salted water to a boil and cook the pasta for about 10 minutes or until just tender. Rinse in cold water and drain well.
2 Turn the pasta into a large bowl and stir in the prepared fruit, celery and salami. Mix thoroughly to ensure ingredients are well combined.
3 To make the dressing: mix together the mayonnaise, orange juice and lemon rind and juice. Beat with a fork until thoroughly combined. Season with salt and pepper.
4 Toss the salad and dressing well together, then turn into a salad bowl and sprinkle over the chives and cashews.
5 Serve garnished with slices of unpeeled orange and watercress.

Cook's Notes

TIME
Preparation of this salad takes 20 minutes plus 10 minutes to cook the pasta.

SERVING IDEAS
This makes a refreshing summer lunch.

●430 calories per portion

97

Hot pasta and sausage salad

SERVES 4

2 cups pasta shells
½ lb garlic sausage, skinned and cut into ½ inch cubes
salt
2 teaspoons vegetable oil
¼ cup quick dried peas
1 small red pepper, seeded and cut into strips
½ cup dairy sour cream
2 tablespoons chopped fresh parsley
freshly ground black pepper

1 Bring a saucepan of salted water to a boil, add the oil, pasta and peas and then cook for 7-8 minutes.

2 Add the sausage and red pepper to the pan and continue cooking for 5 minutes more until the pasta is just cooked.

3 Drain the mixture well, return to the rinsed-out pan and stir in the sour cream, parsley and salt and pepper to taste. Heat through very gently. Transfer the pasta and sausage to a warmed serving dish and serve at once.

Cook's Notes

 TIME
Preparation and cooking take about 25 minutes.

 VARIATIONS
Use 1 cup frozen peas instead of dried, but cook them only for 3-4 minutes. Instead of garlic sausage, use fresh cooked or drained canned sausages or any variety of frankfurters you like.

 SERVING IDEAS
Serve hot with buttered wholemeal bread or toast and a green salad.

 COOK'S TIP
Pasta shells look attractive because of their shape but you can use any other small pasta shapes.

●420 calories per portion

98

Radish and pasta salad

SERVES 4
½ lb radishes
1½ cups pasta spirals or pasta shells
salt
1 teaspoon vegetable oil
2 tablespoons snipped chives
½ cup dairy sour cream
freshly ground black pepper

1 Bring a large pan of salted water to a boil, swirl in the oil, then add the pasta. Bring back to a boil and cook, uncovered, for 10-15 minutes until tender but firm to the bite. Drain the pasta thoroughly in a strainer, then rinse well under cold running water, to remove any excess starch and to cool down the pasta. Drain again thoroughly and leave on one side.

2 Trim the top and bottom of the radishes and cut into 3-4 slices.

3 Transfer the pasta to a serving dish and add the radishes, chives, sour cream and salt and pepper to taste. Toss the salad well and serve at once, while still fresh.

 Cook's Notes

 TIME
This salad only takes about 25 minutes to prepare and assemble.

SERVING IDEAS
Serve as a lunch dish with a green salad. Alternatively, line 6 individual plates or dishes with crisp lettuce leaves, pile the salad in the center of each and serve as a tasty appetizer accompanied by hot garlic or herb bread.

 VARIATIONS
If fresh chives are not available, use the green part of scallions or a few leaves of watercress instead.
Plain yogurt may be used instead of sour cream.

●180 calories per portion

Lamb and mint pasta salad

SERVES 4
¾-1 lb cooked lamb, sliced
salt
1 teaspoon vegetable oil
1 cup pasta rings (see Buying guide)
1 large onion, sliced
mint sprigs, for garnish

MINT DRESSING
2 tablespoons chopped fresh mint
2 tablespoons capers, finely chopped
2 tablespoons vegetable oil
4½ teaspoons white wine vinegar
2 teaspoons sugar
good pinch of dry mustard
salt and freshly ground black pepper

1 Bring a pan of salted water to a boil, swirl in the oil and add the pasta. Cook for 5 minutes, then add the onion slices and cook for 5

Cook's Notes

TIME
Total preparation time for this lamb and pasta salad is about 25 minutes.

SERVING IDEAS
The salad can be prepared in advance and refrigerated until needed. It is a meal in itself, but for a more filling lunch or supper serve with a watercress, ripe olive and orange salad and hot garlic or herb bread.

● 520 calories per portion

VARIATIONS
The onion can be omitted and chopped scallions added to the finished salad instead. Substitute 2 teaspoons concentrated mint sauce for the fresh mint.

BUYING GUIDE
Pasta rings, or *anelli*, are available in yellow or brown. Both types of rings are made from hard durum wheat. The brown rings are made from wholemeal flour which gives them their distinctive color.

minutes more until the pasta is tender but firm to the bite.
2 Meanwhile, make the dressing: put the chopped mint into a large bowl with the capers, oil, vinegar, sugar and mustard. Season to taste with salt and pepper and beat to mix well together.
3 Drain the pasta and onion, rinse under cold running water, then

drain again very thoroughly. Add to the mint and caper dressing and stir well until the pasta and onion are evenly coated.
4 Arrange the cooked lamb in the center of a large serving platter, spoon the pasta salad around the meat and then garnish with mint sprigs. Serve the dish at once (see Serving ideas).

Curried rice salad

SERVES 6
½ cup short-grain or Italian rice
salt
1 can (6 oz) pimientos, drained
1 green pepper, seeded and
    chopped
2 tomatoes, peeled, seeded and
    chopped
2 scallions, thinly sliced
2 tablespoons blanched almonds,
    roughly chopped
¼ cup drained whole corn kernels
1 tablespoon seedless raisins
1 tablespoon golden raisins
margarine or butter, for greasing
watercress sprigs, for garnish

DRESSING
5 tablespoons olive oil
1 tablespoon red wine vinegar
2 teaspoons lemon juice
1 clove garlic, crushed (optional)
1 teaspoon sugar
1 teaspoon mild curry powder

1 Cook the rice in a large pan of
boiling salted water for 10-12 minutes, until it is just tender. Drain the
rice in a strainer, rinse under cold
running water, drain again and turn
into a large bowl.
2 Chop one of the canned pimientos. Cut the remaining ones into
long strips about ½ inch thick and
reserve for the garnish.
3 Stir the chopped pimiento into
the rice, together with the green
pepper, tomatoes, scallions,
almonds, corn kernels, raisins and
golden raisins. Mix well together so
that the vegetables and fruit are
distributed evenly.
4 Make the dressing: put all the
dressing ingredients into a screw-
top jar, add salt to taste and shake
well. Mix the dressing into the rice
mixture.
5 Pack the rice mixture into a 3-cup
pudding mold, pushing it firmly
down with the back of a large
spoon. Cover the bowl with plastic
wrap and set aside to cool.
6 Unmold the rice salad on to a
plate (see Cook's tip). Arrange
pimiento on the top in a wheel
pattern and garnish with watercress. Serve with any cold meat or
as part of a buffet.

Cook's Notes

TIME
Total preparation and cooking time of this dish is 30 minutes.

COOK'S TIP
To unmold the rice salad, run a thin-bladed knife around the inside of the mold to loosen it. Put a flat serving plate over the mold and, holding the two firmly together, invert the mold. Give a sharp shake to release the rice. Stand the plate on a surface and lift off the mold, taking care not to damage the rice shape.

PREPARATION
To peel the tomatoes, cover them with boiling water and leave for 1 minute; then plunge into cold water. Stab a tomato with a fork, re-move from the water and peel away the skin with a sharp knife. Repeat with the others.

●215 calories per portion

Brown rice ring

SERVES 4
⅔ cup brown rice
salt
1 red pepper, seeded and diced (see Preparation)
1 green pepper, seeded and diced
2 tablespoons butter or margarine
1 Bermuda onion, chopped
½ lb tomatoes, skinned, seeded and chopped
½ small cucumber, diced (see Cook's tip)

DRESSING
3 tablespoons vegetable oil
1 teaspoon wine vinegar or lemon juice
pinch of dry mustard
pinch of sugar
salt and freshly ground black pepper

1 Rinse the rice and put it into a large saucepan of boiling salted water. Bring to a boil again, reduce heat and simmer, very gently, for about 40 minutes, until the rice is cooked and has absorbed all the water. If necessary, add more boiling water during cooking. Rinse under cold running water and leave in a strainer to drain thoroughly.

2 Meanwhile, soften the diced peppers slightly by plunging them into boiling water for 30 seconds. Drain and refresh immediately under cold running water.

3 Melt the butter in a skillet, add the onion and cook over gentle heat for 5 minutes until it is limp and translucent. Remove from the heat and stir in the peppers, tomatoes and cucumber.

4 Put the ingredients for the dressing in a large bowl and beat with a fork to blend thoroughly.

5 Add the drained rice to the dressing with the vegetables and gently mix all the ingredients together, using 2 forks. Pack into a 1-quart plain ring mold and refrigerate for at least 1 hour.

6 To unmold: run a knife around the ring mold. Invert a serving plate on top and give the mold a sharp tap. Serve chilled.

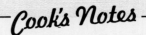

Cook's Notes

 TIME
The rice takes about 40 minutes to cook. Preparation time for the vegetables is about 15 minutes. Allow at least 1 hour for chilling the mold before serving.

 PREPARATION
Cut the vegetables into small neat dice to give the dish an attractive finish.

 SERVING IDEAS
This rice salad makes a good vegetarian snack as it is. If you want to serve it as a salad accompaniment at a buffet supper, fill the center with watercress and garnish the sides with sliced pimiento-stuffed olives, slices of cucumber or tomato and twists of lemon. Or make a spectacular main-course salad by filling the center with a mixture of shrimp and mayonnaise sprinkled with paprika.

 VARIATIONS
Try adding a few pignoli and chopped raisins, chopped walnuts or cooked kidney beans to the rice mixture. Or use 8 dill pickles instead of the cucumber.

! **WATCHPOINT**
Brown rice does take considerably longer than white to cook and different types of rice will absorb varying amounts of water. So, for this reason, keep an eye on the rice while it is cooking and add some more water if necessary. Simmer gently over low to medium heat; if it cooks too quickly, the water will evaporate before the rice is cooked.

 COOK'S TIP
If you have time, put the peeled, diced cucumber in a strainer, sprinkle with salt and leave for 1 hour to draw out the juices. Rinse and pat dry with kitchen paper.

●310 calories per portion

Chicken and zucchini salad

SERVES 4
2 cups diced chicken meat, cut into
   bite-sized pieces
1½ cups long-grain rice
2 tablespoons vegetable oil
¾ lb zucchini, thickly sliced
2 teaspoons curry powder
1½ tablespoons lemon juice
salt and freshly ground black
   pepper
2 tablespoons thick mayonnaise
2 bananas

1 Bring a pan of salted water to a boil and cook the rice for 12-15 minutes until just tender. Rinse well under cold running water to separate the grains. Drain well and set aside for 30 minutes until cold.
2 Meanwhile, heat half the oil in a skillet and sauté the zucchini and curry powder briskly for about 4-5 minutes, turning, until golden and cooked through. Remove from pan with a slotted spoon and drain on absorbent paper.

3 Put 1 tablespoon of the lemon juice and the remaining oil in a large serving bowl, season to taste with salt and pepper and mix well. Stir in the cold rice and zucchini, forking the dressing through them evenly.
4 Put mayonnaise into a separate bowl. Add the cooked chicken pieces and stir them into the mayonnaise until well coated.
5 Fold the chicken into the rice mixture until evenly distributed. Peel and slice the bananas and arrange on top, then sprinkle with the remaining lemon juice. Serve at once (see Serving ideas).

Cook's Notes

TIME
Total preparation and cooking time for the dish is 1 hour.

WATCHPOINT
The zucchini should be only just tender; if they are overcooked and too soft they will break up and spoil the appearance of the salad.

SERVING IDEAS
Sprinkle this hearty salad with a little lightly toasted flaked coconut and garnish with a border of lemon slices.

VARIATIONS
Use chunks of cooked ham instead of chicken and, if liked, add chopped, well-drained canned pineapple pieces.

●515 calories per portion

103

Turkey and ham salad

SERVES 4
1 cup diced cooked turkey, cut into bite-sized pieces
1½ cups diced cooked ham
1 cup long-grain rice
salt
1 small red pepper, seeded and chopped
5 scallions, chopped
4 tablespoons thick mayonnaise
3 tablespoons plain yogurt
1 clove garlic, crushed (optional)
freshly ground black pepper
¼ lb grapes, halved, seeds removed
3 ripe Chinese gooseberries, peeled and sliced (see Buying guide and Preparation)
lettuce leaves, to serve

1 Cook the rice in plenty of boiling salted water for 12-15 minutes until tender, then rinse well under cold running water to separate the grains.
2 Put the drained rice into a large bowl, add the turkey, ham, pepper and scallions and fold in gently.
3 In a small bowl, mix together the mayonnaise, yogurt and garlic, if using, and season with salt and pepper. Pour over the rice mixture and fold to mix again.
4 Gently stir the grapes and Chinese gooseberries into the salad. Cover and keep in a cool place until ready to serve.
5 To serve: pile the salad on a bed of lettuce.

Cook's Notes

 TIME
The salad takes about 30 minutes to prepare.

 VARIATIONS
Other salad vegetables can be used in this salad – sliced stuffed olives and sliced raw button mushrooms look particularly attractive. Try using about a cup of chopped fresh pineapple instead of the Chinese gooseberries.

 BUYING GUIDE
Chinese gooseberry, or Kiwifruit, has a furry brown skin and translucent bright green flesh; it is available from midsummer right through until winter from good farm markets and larger supermarkets. To test if ripe, squeeze the fruit gently with your fingers – it should be soft to the touch. If the fruit are not ripe when you buy them, place them in a bag with an apple and leave for a few days at room temperature.

 PREPARATION
To peel and slice Chinese gooseberries:

Using a vegetable parer or small, sharp knife, peel the skin off the fruit lengthwise in thin strips. Slice the peeled fruit crossways into thin rounds.

●495 calories per portion

Greek rice ring

SERVES 4
¾ cup long-grain rice
1 cup small ripe olives, pitted
salt
¾ cup diced cooked lamb
½ cup stuffed green olives, sliced
2 tomatoes, diced
1 green pepper, seeded and cut into
   ½-inch pieces (see Cook's tips)
2 tablespoons olive oil
1 tablespoon lemon juice
1 teaspoon chopped fresh mint
½ teaspoon dried oregano
freshly ground black pepper
margarine, for greasing

1 Preheat oven to 350°.
2 Lightly grease a 1-quart plain ring mold with margarine (see Cook's tips) and arrange the ripe olives evenly around the base.
3 Bring a pan of salted water to a boil and cook the rice for 15 minutes or until it is tender but still firm to the bite. Drain well, but do not rinse as the starch is necessary in this instance to hold the rice together when the rice is de-molded.
4 Put the rice into a large bowl and mix thoroughly with the remaining ingredients. Season to taste with salt and ground black pepper.
5 Spoon mixture into prepared ring mold and press down lightly. Cover with greased foil, then bake in the oven for 25 minutes. Turn out on to a warmed serving platter, remove the ring mold and serve at once (see Serving ideas).

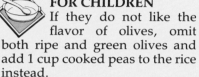

Cook's Notes

 TIME
Preparation time is about 15 minutes and cooking time 45-50 minutes.

COOKS TIPS
If pepper pieces are any larger than recommended here, they may cause ring to break up when unmolded.
   If a ring mold is unavailable, use a 7-inch solid-based round cake pan instead.

 VARIATIONS
Instead of lamb, use cold, cooked, chicken.

 FOR CHILDREN
If they do not like the flavor of olives, omit both ripe and green olives and add 1 cup cooked peas to the rice instead.

SERVING IDEAS
Serve the rice ring hot on its own, or leave to cool and serve cold. For a buffet lunch, serve with a Greek salad of Feta cheese, onions and tomatoes piled in the center of the rice ring.

●305 calories per portion

DESSERTS

Mediterranean rice dessert

SERVES 4-6
⅓ cup long-grain rice
4 cups milk
⅓ cup sugar
grated rind of 1 lemon
2 egg yolks
1 cup heavy whipping cream
grated semi-sweet chocolate,
    to decorate

1 Put rice, milk, sugar and lemon rind in a heavy-bottomed saucepan. Bring to a boil, then reduce heat and simmer for 50 minutes until thick and creamy. Keep the heat very low and stir the rice gently from time to time to prevent sticking.

2 In a small bowl, beat the egg yolks and cream together until blended. Beat in about ¼ cup of the hot rice mixture, then stir this into rice mixture in the pan. Cook over a low heat for about 2 minutes, stirring. Do not let the rice mixture boil.

3 Remove the pan from the heat and pour the pudding into 4 individual dessert bowls. Sprinkle a little grated chocolate over each pudding. Serve hot or chilled.

Cook's Notes

TIME
Preparation and cooking take about 60 minutes. Remember to allow chilling time if serving cold.

DID YOU KNOW
This type of pudding is popular in the Mediterranean, where it is often served sprinkled with cinnamon. Alternatively you could decorate the rice with fresh, canned or crystallized fruits.

●185 calories per portion

106

Polish noodle dessert

SERVES 4-6
½ lb tagliatelle (see Buying guide)
3 tablespoons poppy seeds (see
  Economy)
2 tablespoons clear honey
½ teaspoon vanilla
salt
2 tablespoons melted butter
1 cup seedless raisins

1 Put the poppy seeds into a bowl, cover with boiling water and leave to soak for 3 hours.
2 Drain the poppy seeds in a fine strainer, then press gently to extract as much liquid as possible. Spread the poppy seeds over a clean dishtowel and pat dry.
3 Put the poppy seeds into a large bowl. Add the honey and vanilla and mash together with a wooden

spoon to make a thick black paste. Make sure the ingredients are thoroughly mixed together.
4 Bring a large pan of salted water to a boil, add the tagliatelle and stir once. Bring back to a boil and cook for about 7 minutes, until the tag-

liatelle is *al dente* (tender, yet firm to the bite). Drain well.
5 Add the tagliatelle to the poppy seed paste with the melted butter and raisins. Mix together well using 2 forks and serve at once (see Serving ideas).

Cook's Notes

 TIME
3 hours soaking for the poppy seeds, then 45 minutes preparation.

 DID YOU KNOW
In Poland, this dish is traditionally served on Christmas Eve.

WATCHPOINT
It is important to mash the ingredients thoroughly as this releases the particularly distinctive flavor of the poppy seeds.

 BUYING GUIDE
Buy yellow tagliatelle (also called egg noodles) for this dessert.

 ECONOMY
It is less expensive to buy poppy seeds loose from a delicatessen than in jars.

 SERVING IDEAS
Although not traditional, dairy sour cream makes a good accompaniment.

●450 calories per portion

Imperial rice mold

SERVES 6-8
1 envelope unflavored gelatin
¾ cup red fruit juice
sugar, if required
⅓ cup long-grain rice
4 cups milk
3 tablespoons sugar
1 teaspoon vanilla
3 tablespoons water
½ cup candied cherries, quartered
2 tablespoons golden raisins
2 tablespoons diced candied angelica
2 egg whites
½ cup heavy whipping cream

1 Rinse out a 6-cup metal jelly mold with cold water, then shake off the excess moisture. Soak 1 teaspoon of gelatin in the fruit juice in a cup for 5 minutes. Put the cup in a pan of hot water and stir gelatin until dissolved. Stir in sugar to taste. Pour into mold, cover and refrigerate until set.

2 Make the rice mold: put rice, milk, sugar and vanilla in a heavy-bottomed pan. Bring to a boil, then reduce heat and simmer for 50 minutes until thick and creamy.

3 Dissolve remaining gelatin in the 3 tablespoons water as in step 1. Stir into the hot rice with the cherries, raisins and angelica. Cover and chill, stirring occasionally, until on the point of setting.

4 In a clean, dry bowl, beat the egg whites until standing in stiff peaks. Beat the cream until it forms soft peaks. Using a large metal spoon, fold the cream and then the egg whites into the rice mixture.

5 Spoon the mixture into the mold, over the jelly, cover and return to the refrigerator for 2-3 hours, until set (see Cook's tip).

6 Unmold the dessert. Loosen edges with a palette knife then dip mold in hot water for 1-2 seconds. Invert a dampened plate on top then, holding mold and plate together, invert them giving a sharp shake halfway round. Lift off mold and mop up any liquid from plate. Leave at room temperature for 30 minutes, to take the chill off the flavor, before serving.

108

Cook's Notes

 TIME
60 minutes preparation, plus setting time.

 SPECIAL OCCASION
Spoon half the red jelly into the mold and chill until on the point of setting. Press slices of banana and 'diamonds' of angelica into the almost-set jelly in a decorative pattern. Spoon over the remaining jelly and return to the refrigerator to set.

 COOK'S TIP
The dessert can be prepared ahead up to the end of stage 5 and kept, covered, in the refrigerator for up to 24 hours.

! **WATCHPOINT**
Do not let the mixture become too stiff at stage 3, or it will be hard to incorporate the egg whites and cream.

●310 calories per portion

Date rice

SERVES 4
¼ cup long-grain rice
2½ cups milk
1 tablespoon butter or margarine
⅓ cup chopped dates (see Buying guide)
grated rind of 1 orange
melted margarine, for greasing

1 Preheat oven to 300°. Brush the inside of a 1-quart flameproof dish with melted margarine, spreading this evenly round the sides..
2 Put the rice, milk and butter into a saucepan. Bring just to boiling point, then remove from the heat. Stir in the chopped dates and grated orange rind. Pour into the prepared flameproof dish and place the dish on a cookie sheet.
3 Bake in the oven for about 2 hours, or until the rice is tender and most of the milk has been absorbed. Serve hot (see Serving ideas).

Cook's Notes

TIME
Preparation 20 minutes, cooking time 2 hours.

ECONOMY
If you are using the oven heated to 325° for a main dish, the dessert may be baked on the bottom shelf.

VARIATIONS
Use other dried fruits, such as raisins or currants in place of some or all of the dates. For added flavor, grate a little nutmeg over the top.

BUYING GUIDE
Buy dates that are already pitted and chopped – available from most supermarkets.

SERVING IDEAS
Serve hot, topped with fresh orange sections, or drained, canned mandarins.

COOK'S TIP
Heating the milk and rice first helps to keep baking time to a minimum.

●220 calories per portion

Rich rice pudding

SERVES 4
1 cup short-grain rice
2½ cups milk
finely grated rind of ½ orange
⅓ cup sugar
2 tablespoons butter
3 egg yolks, beaten
½ cup thin cream
butter, for greasing

1 Preheat oven to 350°. Generously butter a 5-cup flameproof dish (see Cook's tip).

2 Put the rice in a saucepan with the milk and orange rind. Bring slowly to a boil. Cook, stirring occasionally, for 15-20 minutes, until rice is just tender.

3 Turn the heat off under the rice, add the sugar and butter and stir until melted. Let the rice mixture cool for 5 minutes. Thoroughly stir in the beaten egg yolks, then the cream.

4 Pour into the prepared dish and bake in the oven for about 40 minutes, stirring thoroughly 3 times during cooking. At the end of cooking the pudding will have a thin skin and most of the liquid will have been absorbed. Serve warm, from the dish.

Cook's Notes

TIME
Preparation about 25 minutes, cooking 40 minutes. Cooling 5 minutes.

COOK'S TIP
Choose a fairly deep, wide dish.

SERVING IDEAS
Serve on its own or accompanied with stewed fruit. Or top each portion with a thick fruit preserve.

●465 calories per portion

110

Eastern milk puddings

SERVES 6
1 tablespoon cornstarch
2 tablespoons ground rice
2½ cups milk
¼ cup sugar
2-3 teaspoons rosewater
⅓ cup ground almonds
1 tablespoon chopped pistachio
   nuts, to decorate

1 Put the cornstarch and rice in a bowl and mix with a little milk, stirring everything together.

2 Pour the remaining milk into a saucepan, add the sugar and heat until the sugar has dissolved and the milk is almost at boiling point. Pour the milk on to the paste, stirring constantly, then return to the pan and bring slowly to simmering point, stirring all the time.

3 Simmer gently for about 8 minutes, stirring constantly until the mixture begins to thicken slightly and coats the back of the spoon.

4 Add the rosewater and cook, stirring, for 2 minutes, then beat in the almonds with a wire whisk until smooth. Remove from heat.

5 Pour the custard into 6 individual dishes. Allow to cool, then cover and refrigerate for 2 hours until firm. Decorate with the chopped pistachio nuts just before serving.

Cook's Notes

 TIME
20 minutes preparation, plus 2 hours chilling.

 VARIATION
If pistachios are not available, use walnuts or almonds instead.

● 150 calories per portion

Rhubarb rice mold

SERVES 4-6
1/3 cup long-grain rice
3 cups milk
1 cup half-and-half
1/2 teaspoon vanilla
3 tablespoons sugar
1 can (about 1 lb) rhubarb, drained
   and syrup reserved
1 envelope unflavored gelatin

1 Put rice, milk, half-and-half, vanilla and sugar in a heavy-bottomed pan. Bring to a boil, then reduce the heat and simmer for 50 minutes until thick and creamy. Put on one side until cold.

2 Rinse out a 5-cup mold with cold water, shake off the excess moisture, then refrigerate.

3 Put drained rhubarb and rice in a large bowl and beat to mix.

4 Sprinkle the gelatin over the reserved rhubarb syrup in a flameproof bowl. Leave to soak for 5 minutes, then stand the bowl in a pan of gently simmering water for 1-2 minutes, stirring occasionally, until the gelatin has dissolved.

5 Cool the gelatin slightly, then pour it in a thin stream on to the rhubarb mixture, stirring constantly. Spoon the mixture into the prepared mold, cover with plastic wrap and refrigerate until set.

6 To unmold the dessert: loosen the edges of the mixture from the sides of the mold with your fingers. Dip the mold into a bowl of hot water for 1-2 seconds, then invert a dampened plate on top. Hold the mold and plate firmly and invert, giving a sharp shake. Lift off the mold.

Cook's Notes

 TIME
60 minutes preparation, plus 3-4 hours setting time and 30 minutes standing at room temperature.

 COOK'S TIP
Using canned rhubarb makes this an easy-to-prepare dessert. If you want to make it with fresh rhubarb, place 2 cups trimmed, chopped stalks in an enamel or other lined saucepan. Add 1/2 cup water and sugar to taste, then cover and cook gently until the rhubarb is tender. Cool completely, then drain well, reserving 1/2 cup of the cooking liquid.

●190 calories per portion

Flaky rice sundae

SERVES 4
2½ cups milk
¼ cup flaked rice (see Buying guide)
2 tablespoons sugar
few drops of vanilla

TOPPING
1 tablespoon butter or margarine
1 tablespoon corn syrup
1 cup corn flakes or rice crispies

1 Pour the milk into a medium heavy-bottomed saucepan. Bring slowly to simmering point over low heat, then sprinkle in the flaked rice. Simmer gently, stirring frequently, for 15-20 minutes, until the rice is tender and thickened.
2 Remove from the heat and stir in the sugar and vanilla, to taste. Cool slightly, then spoon into 4 dessert

dishes. Leave to cool completely.
3 Make the topping: melt the butter with the syrup in a saucepan over low heat. Remove from the heat, add the corn flakes and stir gently

with a large metal spoon until evenly coated.
4 Spoon the topping over the dessert. Leave to set about 30 minutes before serving.

Cook's Notes

TIME
35 minutes preparation, plus cooling time.

BUYING GUIDE
You can buy white and brown rice flakes. The brown variety, which are sold in health food stores, have a pleasant 'nutty' flavor and more food value.

WATCHPOINTS
The milk should only simmer gently, otherwise it will evaporate and the dessert will be too thick.

The topping sticks together and hardens as it cools, so it

must be divided between the dishes while still warm.

SERVING IDEAS
This easy-to-make milk dessert with its tempting crisp, sweet topping can also be served hot. Spoon the dessert into the dishes, but do not cool; make and add the topping, then serve at once.

VARIATIONS
Try this topping over other milk puddings, such as semolina or a vanilla pudding.

●240 calories per portion

Peach rice condé

SERVES 6
⅓ cup pudding rice, rinsed and
   well drained
¼ cup sugar
5 cups milk
1¼ cups heavy whipping cream
½ teaspoon vanilla
¼ cup red jelly
1 can (about 1½ lb) peach halves,
   well drained

1 Put the rice, sugar and milk into a large saucepan. Partially cover the pan and cook over very low heat for about 1 hour, stirring regularly, until the rice is soft and has absorbed almost all of the milk.
2 Pour the cooked rice into a large bowl. Cover the surface closely with plastic wrap to prevent a skin forming, then set the rice aside to cool

TIME
30 minutes preparation, about 1 hour cooking, plus several hours cooling, preferably overnight.

VARIATIONS
Canned pears, apricots or pineapple can be used instead of peaches.

COOK'S TIP
Prepare the rice up to the end of stage 2 the day before you intend serving

the dessert. Keep it in the refrigerator until ready to finish.

! WATCHPOINT
The rice must be stirred frequently during the cooking to prevent it sticking. The cooked rice should be creamy and thick enough to support the weight of the peaches, if it is too runny, drain off all the surplus liquid before cooling.

●485 calories per portion

completely (see Cook's tip).
3 Beat the cream until it forms soft peaks. Fold half of the cream and the vanilla into the cold rice, then spoon evenly into a serving dish.
4 Put the red jelly into a small saucepan and heat gently until melted. Remove from the heat.

5 Arrange the peach halves, cut side down, on top of the rice, leaving a small border around the edge. Brush the peaches with the warmed jelly.
6 Pipe or spoon the remaining cream neatly around the edge of the rice and in the center. Serve cold.

Creamy Danish rice

SERVES 4-6
½ cup short-grain or pudding rice
2 cups half-and-half (see Buying guide)
1½ tablespoons sugar
1 cup heavy whipping cream
½ cup finely chopped almonds
1 teaspoon vanilla
1 tablespoon cream sherry (optional)

1 Bring the milk slowly to a boil in a heavy-bottomed saucepan. Add the rice and sugar and stir well. Cover the pan and cook as gently as possible for about 45 minutes, stirring frequently, until the rice is cooked and tender.

2 Turn the cooked rice into a wide bowl and leave until completely cold, stirring occasionally to prevent a skin forming on top.

3 Beat the cream until it just forms soft peaks. Using a large metal spoon, fold the cream into the rice, then fold in the almonds, reserving 1 tablespoon for decoration. Fold in the vanilla and sherry, if using.

4 Spoon the mixture into a serving dish, cover and refrigerate for at least 30 minutes. Serve the pudding chilled, sprinkled with the reserved almonds (see Serving ideas).

Cook's Notes

TIME
Preparation takes about 40 minutes, but allow about 2 hours for the rice to cool and at least 30 minutes chilling time for the pudding.

WATCHPOINT
Keep an eye on the rice, especially towards the end of cooking time, and stir regularly to prevent it sticking. When cooked, the rice should be soft, but not mushy.

DID YOU KNOW

In Denmark this rice pudding is traditionally served on Christmas Eve. A whole blanched almond may be buried in the pudding just before it is served: the person who finds it is given a present and the belief is that if a young girl finds it she will soon marry.

SERVING IDEAS

Serve the dessert with poached fruit, or with a tart fresh fruit to offset its creamy richness.

BUYING GUIDE

Ordinary milk can be used instead of half-and-half, but will give a slightly less rich result.

●375 calories per portion

115

Quick peach crisp

SERVES 4

1 can (about 1¾ lb) peach slices, drained, syrup reserved
1 cup crispy rice cereal, lightly crushed (see Cook's tips)
⅓ cup light soft brown sugar
5 tablespoons butter or margarine, melted
2 tablespoons all-purpose flour
¾ teaspoon ground mixed spice
pinch of salt

1 Preheat oven to 350°.
2 Put the peaches and 2 tablespoons reserved syrup into a 5-cup flameproof dish.
3 Mix together the remaining ingredients and sprinkle over the peaches. Press down lightly.
4 Bake in the oven for 30 minutes until golden. Serve hot.

Cook's Notes

TIME
Preparation 15 minutes, cooking time about 30 minutes.

COOK'S TIPS
Crush the crispy rice cereal by squeezing handfuls of them in your fist.
This dessert is useful as it can be quickly made from store-cupboard ingredients.

VARIATIONS
Use other canned fruit, such as apricots, mangoes, mandarin oranges or pears.

SERVING IDEAS
Serve with dairy sour cream, plain yogurt or vanilla ice cream.

ECONOMY
Save the extra syrup and use it for a fruit salad. Alternatively, freeze it in special containers, to make unusual ice lollipops for children.

●295 calories per portion

Crispie gâteau

MAKES 6-8 SLICES
5 cups crispie rice cereal
6 tablespoons butter
1 cup marshmallows
⅓ cup toffee sugar candies
vegetable oil, for greasing

FILLING
½ tablespoon unflavored gelatin
3 tablespoons water
2 cups cold milk (see Watchpoints)
2 × 3⅛ oz butterscotch pudding mix
2 small bananas
1 teaspoon lemon juice
1 can (about ½ lb) peach slices, drained

1 Lightly oil an 8-inch springform cake pan. Put the rice cereal into a large bowl.
2 Put the butter, marshmallows and toffee candies into a heavy-bottomed pan. Heat gently, stirring occasionally, until melted, then beat until smooth. Pour on to the rice cereal and mix until evenly blended.
3 With the back of a large metal spoon press the cereal mixture evenly over the bottom and sides of the prepared pan. Leave in a cool place for at least 2 hours to firm.
4 Make the filling: sprinkle the gelatin over the water in a small heatproof bowl. Leave to soak for 5 minutes, then stand bowl in a pan of gently simmering water for 1-2 minutes, stirring occasionally, until gelatin has dissolved. Remove bowl from pan.
5 Pour the milk into a large bowl and beat in butterscotch mixes. Leave for 1 minute until thickened, then fold in gelatin.
6 Slice the bananas, then cut each slice across into 3 strips. Toss in lemon juice, then fold into butterscotch mixture. Refrigerate for 1 hour, or until on point of setting.
7 Carefully remove cereal case from pan and place on a serving plate. Turn butterscotch mixture into case and level the surface. Leave in a cool place for about 1 hour, until set. Arrange the peach slices over the filling and serve at once.

Cook's Notes

TIME
45 minutes preparation, plus 2 hours for the case to firm and a further 2 hours for the filling to set.

WATCHPOINTS
Use whole milk, or the mixes will not thicken. Do not assemble the gâteau more than 1 hour before serving or the crispie case will soften.

SERVING IDEAS
This dessert-cum-cake is ideal for a tea-party; tie a ribbon around the sides for a more festive look.

●490 calories per slice

117

Chocolate nutty tapioca

SERVES 4
3 tablespoons quick-cooking
  tapioca (see Did you know)
2½ cups milk
2 tablespoons light soft brown
  sugar

TOPPING
1 oz raw peanuts, coarsely chopped
1 square (1 oz) semi-sweet
  chocolate, coarsely grated

1 Put the tapioca into a medium heavy-bottomed pan and mix in the milk. Let stand for 5 minutes to allow the grains to swell a little.
2 Cook over medium heat, stirring constantly until the mixture comes to a full boil. Remove from the heat – the mixture should be thick and creamy. Mix in the sugar stirring until it has dissolved.
3 Heat the broiler to medium.
4 Turn the tapioca mixture into a shallow, flameproof dish. Level the surface, then sprinkle with the chopped peanuts and grated chocolate. Broil for 1-2 minutes, until the chocolate is melted and the nuts are lightly browned.
5 Serve the pudding hot or cold or just slightly warm.

Cook's Notes

 TIME
This easy-to-make dessert takes just over 1 hour to prepare and cook.

 DID YOU KNOW
Tapioca comes from the root of the cassava plant, widely grown in the West Indies. It is sold in the form of medium or tiny pearls as well as flakes. Because of its high starch content it will absorb more liquid than some other grains, and is sometimes also used in savory dishes such as soups or stews to thicken them.

●235 calories per portion

118

Blueberry semolina

SERVES 4
2½ cups milk
2-inch piece stick cinnamon
¼ cup caster sugar
⅓ cup semolina
2 egg yolks

TO FINISH
1 can (about 1 lb) blueberries
2 tablespoons heavy cream

1 Pour 2 cups of the milk into a heavy-bottomed saucepan. Add the cinnamon stick, then stir in the sugar. Bring almost to a boil, then remove from the heat, cover and leave for 20 minutes to allow the milk to absorb the flavor of the cinnamon stick.

2 Put the semolina into a large bowl and slowly stir in the remaining milk, mixing well. Using a wire whisk, beat in the egg yolks. Discard the cinnamon from the flavored milk, then gradually stir the milk into the semolina mixture.

3 Pour the mixture into a clean, heavy-bottomed saucepan and stir over very low heat for 5-7 minutes, or until thickened. As soon as the first bubble appears, remove the pan from the heat and continue stirring for a further 2 minutes until the mixture is slightly cooled.

4 Pour the semolina mixture into a 1-quart glass serving bowl. Cover closely with plastic wrap and refrigerate for at least 3 hours, or overnight, to firm.

5 Purée the blueberries and their syrup in a blender, then work purée through a strainer to remove any tough bits of skin. Refrigerate the purée until ready to serve.

6 To serve: uncover the semolina, spread the blueberry purée evenly over the surface, then lightly swirl the cream on the top.

Cook's Notes

TIME
35 minutes preparation (including standing time for the milk), plus at least 3 hours chilling. Allow about 5 minutes to finish.

WATCHPOINT
Stir the semolina mixture constantly during cooking. Do not let it boil, or the egg yolks will scramble.

VARIATIONS
Instead of using a large bowl, divide the semolina mixture between 4 ramekins, or individual glass serving dishes.

Any thick fruit purée can be used instead of blueberry. A slightly tart flavor is best.

●380 calories per portion

INDEX